The Open
Secret of
Strength

Books in this series . . .

Let's Listen to Jesus (John 13–17)
Our Freedom in Christ (Romans)
The Open Secret of Strength (Philippians)
Faith for the Journey (Hebrews)

A BIBLE STUDY ON PHILIPPIANS

The Open Secret of Strength

REUBEN R. WELCH

FRANCIS ASBURY PRESS
of Zondervan Publishing House
Grand Rapids, Michigan

FRANCIS ASBURY PRESS is an imprint of
Zondervan Publishing House
1415 Lake Drive, S. E.
Grand Rapids, Michigan 49506

Library of Congress Cataloging in Publication Data

Welch, Reuben.
    The open secret of strength : a Bible study on Philippians / Reuben R. Welch.
      p.   cm.
    ISBN 0-310-75281-7
    1. Bible. N.T. Philippians—Study. I. Title. II. Series.
BS2705.5.W44   1988
227'.6077—dc19   87-34915
                                                          CIP

Edited by Dimples Kellogg
Designed by Ann Cherryman

Printed in the United States of America

88 89 90 91 92 93 / CH / 9 8 7 6 5 4 3 2 1

CONTENTS

Preface   7

Chapter One (Philippians 1:3–8)
    The Divine Initiative   9

Chapter Two (Philippians 1:9–11)
    A Prayer for All Seasons   20

Chapter Three (Philippians 1:12–18, 20–21)
    To Live Is Christ   31

Chapter Four (Philippians 1:27–30)
    Life Worthy of the Gospel   42

Chapter Five (Philippians 2:1–11)
    The Mind of Christ   53

Chapter Six (Philippians 2:12–18)
    Fear and Trembling   64

Chapter Seven (Philippians 2:19–30)
    Ordinary Christian Life   73

Chapter Eight (Philippians 3:1–9)
    Loss and Gain   84

Chapter Nine (Philippians 3:7–11)
    Knowing Jesus   94

Chapter Ten (Philippians 3:12–16)
  The Upward Call   105

Chapter Eleven (Philippians 4:4–7)
  Rejoice in the Lord   116

Chapter Twelve (Philippians 4:8–9)
  On Thinking and Doing   125

Chapter Thirteen (Philippians 4:10–13)
  The Open Secret of Strength   135

Preface

● Philippians is a favorite book of almost every Christian and for good reason. Paul had closer personal and emotional ties with the Philippians than with any other of his churches, and in his letter he expresses joy and confidence both in them and in the gospel. The positive tone of the letter is all the more remarkable because it was written from prison.

Philippi was a proud and patriotic city in the Roman province of Macedonia, a little Rome away from Rome. The exciting account of the establishment of the church is found in Acts 16. It includes a "Macedonian call," a women's prayer meeting, a false imprisonment, a night in the stocks, an earthquake, a jailer's conversion, and a town's apology. A thriving, healthy church soon developed that kept close and supportive ties with the apostle all through his missionary travels.

The letter is actually a sort of "thank-you" note. The church heard that Paul was in prison (most probably in Rome, about A.D. 62–64) and sent him a love-gift, carried by Epaphroditus, whom Paul describes as "my brother and fellow soldier, and your messenger and minister to my need" (2:25). Epaphroditus became seriously ill, so much so that Paul feared that he would die. After his recovery by the "mercy" of God (2:27), Paul sent Epaphroditus back with the letter we know as Philippians. In it Paul expresses his hope to send Timothy, his hope for his own release and reunion with them, and his thanks for their gift.

The letter also gives him opportunity to tell the Philippians of his situation, to share with them his relationship with Christ, and to deal with some problems in the church. Nowhere else does Paul reveal more deeply his love for Christ and his concern for the preaching of the gospel of Christ. Whatever motives others may have in their preaching, whether he himself lives or dies, what matters to him is that Christ is proclaimed and the gospel is advanced.

The great hymn of Christ's self-emptying (2:5-11) is used for the purpose of bringing the Philippians to oneness of heart and mind in the Spirit. Paul's harsh words against those who would call them back to circumcision and legalism (3:2) and his exhortation to Euodia and Syntyche to "agree in the Lord" (4:2) express his desire that oneness of the body be preserved at all costs.

The letter also reflects Paul's radiant joy in Christ—even as it reveals his dreadful, uncertain condition. He remembers the Philippians with joy (1:3), rejoices that Christ is preached—regardless of motive (1:18)—and finds joy in their sharing the mind of Christ in humble servanthood (2:2). He rejoices with them even as he is "poured out" for them (2:17), and he rejoices in the gifts they have sent (4:10).

Paul's joy in his hardships reveals his discovery of a wonderful, open secret of strength. It is the secret of total dependency on Christ. The discovery of that open secret is the goal of these theme studies in Philippians.

CHAPTER · 1

The Divine Initiative

I thank my God in all my remembrance of you, always in every prayer of mine for you all making my prayer with joy, thankful for your partnership in the gospel from the first day until now. And I am sure that he who began a good work in you will bring it to completion at the day of Jesus Christ. It is right for me to feel thus about you all, because I hold you to my heart, for you are all partakers with me of grace, both in my imprisonment and in the defense and confirmation of the gospel. For God is my witness, how I yearn for you all with the affection of Christ Jesus (Phil. 1:3–8).

● Paul must have had a wonderful relationship with the Philippians. At times they were not in close contact, but the words he uses here reflect a close and affectionate bond. He remembers them, prays for them with joy, and is thankful for their partnership with him. Their ties go back a long way, and he longs for their fellowship.

The heart of their affectionate friendship, however, is not their human care for one another; it is the love and grace of God. When Paul remembers them, he thanks God, not them. He is thankful for their partnership—in the gospel. Their place in his heart is directly a result of their common sharing of God's grace and the work of extending the gospel. His yearning for them is with "the affection of Christ Jesus."

Paul does not begin this letter, then, by asking, "How are you getting along? Are you going to be all right?" He encourages them with a clear, plain affirmation that is fundamental to all else he wants to say to them: "I am sure that he who began a good work in you will bring it to completion at the day of Jesus Christ" (1:6). There are many things he wants to say to the Philippians in this brief letter. Some are encouraging; some are probing and searching; some call for rejoicing, while others call for repentance and a change of attitude. But in whatever is said, the basic reality is that God has begun a work in their lives and he will finish it.

I believe God wants to say some things through this letter. Some of them are encouraging; some, I have found, are deeply disturbing and probing. Some have called into question the assumptions that I have held for years. But Paul's opening word of assurance makes all the others saving and healing words. If I know God has begun a good work in my life and will see it through, I can hear both his saving word of judgment and his saving word of grace.

• God Is the Initiator

What I see in this passage—and what we will see again and again in the epistle—is a fundamental shift in the center of gravity away from ourselves to God. Here Paul speaks of what theologians have called "the divine initiative." (I wish that phrase sounded as good as it really is. Some words in our religious vocabulary sound almost as holy as they are: *salvation, atonement, redemption, reconciliation,* and so on. One could almost get converted just by listening to them. "The divine initiative" may not have a hallowed sound, but it conveys wonderfully good news.) God is the doer, the initiator, the actor in our affairs. We are the responders, the receivers, and the recipients of his action. This truth is well described by the words of an old hymn:

> I sought the Lord, and afterward I knew
> He moved my soul to seek him, seeking me;
> It was not I that found, O Savior true;
> No, I was found of thee.

Thou didst reach forth thy hand and mine enfold;
I walked and sank not on the storm-vexed sea;
'Twas not so much that I on thee took hold,
As thou, dear Lord, on me.

I find, I walk, I love, but O the whole
Of love is but my answer, Lord, to thee;
For thou wert long beforehand with my soul,
Always thou lovedst me.

I do not know how these words would have fallen on the ears of the Philippians. Theirs was a proud, independent Roman city. But I do know the words do not fall easily upon our ears. It is very hard for us independent, self-sufficient types to hear and accept the fact that God is the initiator in this world.

• God Is True to His Covenant

The entire Bible shows God to be the one who works out his plans and purposes in human history. He is the hero of our story. Let's take a few examples.

The first eleven chapters of Genesis show mankind created in the image of God but fallen and alienated. The four great stories of the Garden, the brothers, the Flood, and the Tower reveal the depth of the human predicament. The first human pair are separated from each other by sin, their children murder, the ground is cursed, and the Flood comes in judgment to destroy the old world. Noah is spared from the Flood, only to fall away from God again. The Tower of Babel symbolizes the confused and alienated condition of mankind.

Then a new kind of history begins; it is saving history initiated by God, not men. God breaks into the wretched situation and says to a very human person named Abram, "I will give you land, and make you a people; I will give you a name and make you a blessing to the families of the whole earth" (see Gen. 12:1–3).

Abram was far from being a perfect example of faith and obedience. We know the story of the famine that sent him to

Egypt, where he tried to pass off his beautiful wife as his sister—to save his own skin. Not a very noble deed. So the pagan Pharaoh lectured the man of God about ethics! God gave Abram the Promised Land, but he offered his shallow nephew the choice of the best property. He was promised a son by his wife, but he couldn't wait, so he fathered Ishmael by a slave girl. The story of Abram/Abraham is the story of God's promise given and threatened. Only the initiative of God preserved it.

Genesis 15 gives us a strange and wonderful story of covenant renewal. It tells us much about the character of the faithful God who takes the initiative to win man back. God tells Abraham to bring before him "a heifer three years old, a she-goat three years old, a ram three years old, a turtledove, and a young pigeon" (Gen. 15:9). Abraham brings these animals before the Lord, cuts them in half and separates the halves, creating a path between them. (In those days, when two persons made a solemn covenant, they walked between the dismembered carcasses to say, "May this happen to us if either of us proves untrue to the covenant.") When night finally came, Abraham watched numb with awe as a smoking fire pot and a burning torch passed between the animals! Those were symbols of God. Abraham did not pass between the carcasses; God did. That is divine initiative.

God makes promises to man, locks himself in to those promises, and keeps them all the way. In this covenant renewal ceremony I see prefigured the Son of God on a cross, making a solemn redeeming covenant with his fallen creatures, binding himself in love to them forever.

Nothing in the Old Testament demonstrates the divine initiative more clearly than the story of Jacob (Gen. 25:29–35:15). He pressured his brother and bought his birthright; he deceived his father and stole the blessing. He fled for his life to Haran, where he lived for twenty years in competition with his uncle, who was almost his match for deviousness.

Finally, Jacob decided to go home—only to hear that his brother Esau, with whom he had made no peace, was marching toward him. To appease him, Jacob sent ahead gifts of flocks and herds. In desperation he divided his people and separated himself from his family. He finally found himself alone in the narrow gorge of the Jabbok River.

Suddenly, a stranger sprang out of the darkness and began wrestling with him. Through the night they struggled, two strong men in fierce competition.

The stranger said, "Let me go, for the day is breaking." Jacob sensed that God was somehow present in the conflict, and he said, "I will not let you go, unless you bless me." The stranger asked, "What is your name?"

It was time for Jacob to own his character-name. "Jacob" meant the deceiver, heel-grasper, and trickster. By saying, "I am Jacob," he was forced to face the truth of who he was. The "enemy" God had been faithful throughout Jacob's fraudulent life, and he was faithful once again.

That was a transforming encounter. Both Jacob's name and his nature were changed. He was no more Jacob, but Israel, which means "God rules." Reconciled to God, he limped on his way toward his brother's reconciling embrace. All his life he had taken his own initiative—against Esau, against his father, against Laban—in an effort to win his God-given destiny. Only the overcoming initiative of God saved him from himself and set him free to fulfill that destiny.

God appeared to Moses on the back slopes of Mount Horeb in a bush that burned. He said, "Go down, tell old Pharaoh, let my people go." God took the initiative to bring down the mighty empire of the Egyptians and set his people free. God performed the mighty deliverance of the Exodus, opening up the waters to bring his people through; he was their wilderness provider and protector. He brought them to Sinai and brought them to himself in covenant love.

And God gave them the land of Canaan. They fought and struggled, failed and conquered, but the battles were the Lord's. A brief paragraph in Exodus 17 tells of a skirmish with the Amalekites, even before the Israelites got to Sinai. As long as Moses held high the rod of God, the Israelites prevailed; but when he grew weary and let down his hands, the enemy prevailed. So Aaron and Hur made a place for Moses to sit, and they held up his arms until the victory was won. That episode doesn't make sense—unless the battle was the Lord's.

Remember the story of the fall of Jericho? The story is so familiar we forget the incredible character of it. Can you visualize the high meeting in the officers' tent? The leader says, "I've got a plan! Let's walk around the place a lot of times and then make all kinds of noise, and the walls will fall down!" Each member of the Joint Chiefs of Staff looks at the others and says, "Why didn't I think of that? Let's do it!" No, the event doesn't make sense—unless the battle was the Lord's.

Then there was Gideon. He was the least of his father's house in the weakest of the clans. The angel of the Lord found him beating out some wheat in the wine press where he was hiding from the Midianites. "The LORD is with you, you mighty man of valor" (Judg. 6:12). So Gideon rallied thirty-two thousand men, whittled them down to three hundred, and lined them up to get their weapons. Each man received a torch, a jar, and a trumpet. Then off they went to fight the Midianites. It doesn't make sense—unless the battle was the Lord's.

Nowhere in the entire settlement narrative does it seem to be significant how many soldiers are available, what weapons they have, or what battle strategies they employ. But it is profoundly significant how obedient the soldiers are, what faith they have, and how they respond to the strategies of God. All through the Old Testament the underlying reality is God's initiative to make and keep his covenant with his people.

Then, in the fullness of time, God "sent forth his Son" to save us (Gal. 4:4). God came to us in Jesus. We did not create the Christ event; we had no part of the redemptive deed on the cross. God called Abram, created a people, delivered them from bondage, judged them when they fell away, and finally sent his own Son as the Savior—long before we were born!

Yet we act as though the whole of salvation rests on our shoulders. Maybe it would be well to pause and reflect that we are not the ones in charge of God's saving activity. We do not begin the good work seen in our lives. God is the originator, and he will see it through.

• God's Good Work in Us

I wonder what the Philippians thought as they heard this statement, which probably was read to them on a Lord's Day morning: "I am sure that he who began a good work in you will bring it to completion. . . ." Was Lydia there? The Holy Spirit had opened her heart to the teachings of the apostles at a prayer meeting down by the river. Her home had become the center of the young church (Acts 16:13–15). Was the church meeting there as Paul's letter was read? What about her business? Did her identification with the new Christian movement make life worse or better for her in the proud Roman city? What about the jailer? Did he hear the apostle's words that day? How did a jailer make a decent living for a Christian family? He probably was glad to be alive (Acts 16:23–34); but what sort of life was it now? And what had happened to the girl, by now a woman, from whom Paul had driven the "spirit of divination" (Acts 16:16–18)?

Perhaps Paul had these individuals in mind as he dictated the words, "I am sure that he who began a good work in you . . . " (Phil. 1:6). He could not forget the day he had seen Christ's transforming revelation on the road to Damascus (Acts 9:1–9), nor could he deny that throughout his life the grace of God had led him, even in his misguided efforts and misdirected zeal. Had he known the words of our hymn, he too would have sung, "For thou wert long beforehand with my soul."

This may seem to be the right time for me to ask, "Has God begun a good work in you?" I thought I would do that, but I have decided against it. Let me tell you why:

Suppose I did ask that question. I don't know how you would answer, but I do know that you would begin thinking . . . about yourself! The center of gravity would remain in your own feelings about yourself. The work of God would be interpreted in terms of human emotions, not in terms of the work of God.

So I will make a declaration instead: *God has indeed begun a good work in you, and he will see it through.* When Paul wrote this declaration to the Philippians, he was not affirming the integrity of their character, the fervency of their religious experience, the orthodoxy of their doctrine, or the steadfastness of their faith. He was making a statement about God. Likewise, I can say that God has begun a good work in you only because it is a statement about God, not about you. This may be the best time in your whole life. It may be the worst time. Perhaps there is no way under heaven for you to think that you will ever be all right or that God has begun doing anything worthwhile in you, let alone see it through!

It is difficult, when we think about such things, to keep from thinking about ourselves. How can I say that God has begun a good work in you when I don't even know you? Truth is, throughout human history God has been faithful to continue his work, in spite of our human weakness and sin. The God who came to us in Jesus his Son is with us in the person of his Holy Spirit, continuing his work of grace, love, redemption, and reconciliation. He is at work in the world, continuing his saving work.

God has begun a good work in each of us. All through our lives he has been present with us, when we have known it and when we have not; when we have said yes and when we have said no; when we have been attentive and when we have been deaf; when we have seen him and when we have been blind. His love and grace have been with us all the way. So when Paul describes our salvation, he does not begin by talking about our response or lack of it. That is another matter. Rather, he begins by talking about God's gracious initiative.

● God's Good Work in the Fellowship

I love this line: "It is right for me to feel thus about you all, because I hold you in my heart, for you are all partakers with me of grace" (1:7). God's good work in my life is not just a matter between God and me; His gracious work in you is not just between God and you. It is a corporate matter, involving the entire fellowship of believers.

The Philippian letter was written to all the Philippian Christians. Paul includes them all in his discussion of the gracious work of God, not just *all* in the sense of everyone, but *all* in the sense of all together.

God's good work is not done in a vacuum; it is accomplished in the fellowship of believers. When Paul says that God has begun a good work "in you," the pronoun is actually plural. This underscores the fact that God's work is done in the context of a fellowship in which, through his Spirit, he continues to work out his good purpose.

There are people around me whom I love and whom I hold in my heart. There are those around me who hold me in their hearts; and so it is with you. When we hold other Christians in our hearts, we do not merely regard them as friends, but as sharers of the grace of God and co-workers in spreading the gospel of God. We have not simply "decided to follow Jesus" on our own and opted to join together to make the journey more enjoyable. God began this good work in us through the ministry of his church; he has caught us up into his saving purposes through his church. And we can be sure he will see his saving purpose through as we live in the context of the church.

I suppose it is too late to make any significant changes in our culturally conditioned way of greeting one another, though it belies the truth of our relationships. We will keep on saying, "How are you?" "How are things going?" "How are you feeling?" and, "Are you all right?" These are good greetings, of course (especially if we wait long enough to hear the answers!). Sometimes, though, I would like to use a new kind of greeting, like "God is working in your life" or "I hold you in my heart." At times those words, said lovingly to me, could make all the difference!

The chorus of a familiar song says, "It is well with my soul." I have come to appreciate those words more since I have understood they are not a testimony to the wellness of my soul, but to the saving grace of God. The point of the songwriter is not that my soul is in great condition; he is not trying to answer the question, "How is your soul?" Rather, he affirms the loving initiative of God. Notice his second verse:

> Though Satan should buffet, though trials should come,
> Let this blest assurance control,
> That Christ hath regarded my helpless estate,
> And hath shed His own blood for my soul.

Because this is true, I can say with confidence, "It is well with my soul." If anyone should ask, "Has God begun a good work in you?" you can answer, "Oh, yes!"

● Discussion Questions

1. Read Acts 16:6–40, which tells of the founding of the Philippian church, the first Christian congregation in Europe. Note the evidence you find in this passage that God was "beginning a good work" in the midst of these people.
2. What words do you find in Philippians 1:3–8 that reflect the kind of relationship Paul had with the Philippians? How would you characterize that relationship?
3. What do you think Paul means by the phrase "from the first day until now"? And what is the "day of Jesus Christ"?
4. Paul is confident that God will continue his good work in the Philippian church. Does this statement suggest that the Philippians had a sense of fear or insecurity about their future? Explain.
5. I have tried to illustrate the initiative that God takes in the salvation process because I believe we think too much about our response to him and we depend too much on our own actions. Do you agree that this is a problem among Christians? Explain.
6. I talk about a "shift in the center of gravity" away from ourselves to God. How would you describe the change that I am recommending in the way we understand our salvation?
7. Do you think the "good work" of God in our lives can be described in any precise way? How would you describe its effect on your life?

8. I think we emphasize the individual's relationship with God and almost ignore our corporate or group relationship with him. Discuss this idea.
9. I have said virtually nothing about our response to the divine initiative. What response do you think Paul expected the Philippians to make? How would you describe the proper response we are to make?
10. How would you react to the greeting "God is at work in your life" or "I hold you in my heart"?

CHAPTER · 2

A Prayer
for All Seasons

And it is my prayer that your love may abound more and more, with knowledge and all discernment, so that you may approve what is excellent, and may be pure and blameless for the day of Christ, filled with the fruits of righteousness which come through Jesus Christ, to the glory and praise of God (Phil. 1:9–11).

● The initiative of God calls for response. Paul expresses that response, not in an exhortation or a command, but in a prayer. It is a specific prayer that flows out of his remembrance of the Philippians, his thankfulness for their fellowship, and his loving care for their welfare. It expresses the real heart concern of the apostle for real persons who were facing problems that could have destroyed the unity and effectiveness of the church.

I think that is why the prayer is so valuable for us. The old and familiar words Paul uses are the very ones we need to sustain and vitalize our own churches. They are not words instructing us to be nicer and kinder and wiser; for all their familiarity, they are strong words that challenge and rebuke us. They are also saving words that can heal and renew us.

The prayer is serious and probing, but it was offered in the overwhelming assurance of God's continuing good work among the Philippians. Paul's intense pastoral concern is mixed with thanksgiving and confidence. The Philippians shared the same grace and lived in the same hope of the completion of God's purposes at the coming of Christ. Therefore it is a prayer of joy.

We need both these attitudes as we study the familiar words of this prayer. If we only hear them superficially, we will miss the probing judgment of God and will not be changed. If we do not hear in them the promise of God's grace and faithfulness, we will only become discouraged.

● A Prayer for Growth in Love

Paul's primary concern is that Christians' "love may abound more and more" (1:9). I read somewhere that the inner fire in the apostle would never let him say, "Now it is enough." Paul's vision of Christ always beckoned him to new insights, new understandings, and new experiences. How many times in his epistles does this theme of "more" appear? Certainly it is found over and over again. I never hear Paul say, "I have been born again and am sure of my salvation," though he certainly was born again and lived in almost exuberant confidence of his relationship with God. He was always pressing on because there was always more knowing and growing in the inexhaustible riches of Christ.

There are Christians who seem to know all there is to know about being a Christian. They know the plan of salvation and have theirs. They know all about what sin is and about who Jesus is and what he has done and how he has done it. They know how to be born again and how to be filled with the Spirit. They know how we are to live and how we are to make life decisions. They know why God does what he does and why he doesn't do what he doesn't do and how to get him to do whatever it is he is supposed to do. Some of them even know all about the Second Coming and how the sequence of final events will unfold.

One cannot deny the logic or the understanding of these Christians, but their facts and the principles are never quite enough to satisfy the deep hunger of the heart for the knowledge of God "which passes all understanding" (4:7). We cry out with Moses, O God, "show my thy glory" (Exod. 33:18), and we bow before the mystery of his being and his ways. We haven't yet begun to know him in the ways he wills to be known and the ways he has made himself present in Christ to be known!

Other Christians are constantly restless in their urgent quest for more answers, more knowledge, or more emotional "highs." They are sure that somewhere there is the answer; someone has the secret, the golden formula to peace without doubts or questions. How many miles, how many dollars are invested by such persons in seminars, conventions, videotapes, and "how-to" books?

I detect neither of these attitudes in Paul. On one side he has total confidence in his relationship with Christ; on the other he is always reaching for maturity in him. And both attitudes are held together by joy and thanksgiving. (The great prayers of Ephesians 1:15–23; 3:14–19 and Colossians 1:9–14; 2:1–5 seem to reveal this same sort of "balanced tension.")

Let's study the great words of this prayer. It begins with the petition "that your love may abound more and more" (1:9). There is no question about the "greatest" thing in the Christian life—it is love (1 Cor. 13). The first fruit of the Spirit (Gal. 5:22–23) has been "poured into our hearts through the Holy Spirit which has been given to us" (Rom. 5:5). It is the "aim of our charge" (1 Tim. 1:5); the "fulfilling of the law" (Rom. 13:10).

Love, however, is never a word that stands alone. It is always used with words that help to define it. All New Testament writers seem to share a common fear that undefined, ungoverned love would degenerate into weak or destructive emotion. They certainly have no fear of emotion, but they do have a profound concern that emotion and love not be understood as synonyms. First Corinthians 13 is valuable precisely because it describes love at length, yet makes no reference to emotion. In Ephesians 1, having heard of the church's love for all the saints, the writer prays for the spirit of wisdom and of revelation in the knowledge of Christ. In Colossians, knowing of that church's love in the Spirit, Paul prays for their knowledge of the will of God in all spiritual wisdom and understanding (1:8–9). His next prayer for them is that their hearts may be knit together in love so that they may have all the riches of assured understanding (2:2).

The same pattern emerges in this Philippian prayer. It is clear that the prayer is for the growth of love. That is exactly what the world needs. But what kind of love? Is it love for God? for one another? for others in general? their love or Christ's love in and through them? The answer to all these is yes.

● Insight Into the Christian Life

Whatever the source of this love or the direction of it, Paul states clearly that it is to "abound more and more in knowledge and all discernment" (1:9). "Knowledge" here does not mean primarily a grasp of the facts about something or someone. Of course, the more we know about the Bible and the life and teachings of Jesus, the more we know about love. We would all agree that the broader our general knowledge of ourselves and our world, the more we are able to understand and practice love. But Paul's prayer is not that we accumulate more facts, but that we enter more deeply into personal relationship with Christ, knowing more and more about who he is and what he can be to us. Our knowledge about the Bible or doctrine or the life and teachings of Jesus leads to a growing, obedient relationship with God in Christ. It includes reflection and enlarged understanding, but always relates to practical life and behavior.

Isaiah said that God's complaint was that "Israel does not know, my people do not understand" (1:3). Gomer, the unfaithful wife of the prophet Hosea, had love for him, no doubt, but she really didn't "know" him; her love did not deepen in knowledge, so it could be seduced. Judas Iscariot had love for Jesus, no doubt, but as we read his story in the Gospels we get the feeling that he really didn't "know" Jesus; he could be enticed to betrayal.

If our own love is not deepened by knowledge, how can it remain vital and compelling in the presence of all the conflicting religious and secular views of our culture? I think of these lines from Eliza Hewitt's gospel song:

> More about Jesus let me learn,
> More of his holy will discern;
> Spirit of God, my teacher be,
> Showing the things of Christ to me.

The word "discernment" indicates perception or discrimination, the ability to make moral decisions. It indicates the practice of testing things with the idea of putting approval on what is best. Our hard decisions are not usually between what is clearly good and what is clearly bad. We mostly struggle between what is good and what is better, or between what is better and what is really the best. Paul understood that such struggles are real. Discernment is not every Christian's gift!

I think knowledge and discernment mean growing understanding and insight into the meaning of Christ and the nature of the Christian life from the perspective of Christ and not of the world. Christians perceive reality differently from the world. Our values are different, our goals are different, and our internal resources are vastly different. The initial response of faith to the saving grace of God does not bring the new perception of reality immediately into focus. We do not suddenly inherit a "Jesus way" of looking at things. We wish we were born into the kingdom with built-in ethical discernment—but we are not!

That is why Paul prayed for a love that would continually grow in understanding and judgment, or wisdom. The truth of the gospel can be overturned by ignorance. God can forgive sin, but what can he do with stupidity? That has seemed to me a serious question. How much subversion of the gospel has come, not from deliberate efforts to sabotage it, but from ignorant efforts to promote it. We are not talking simply about the value of high intelligence; Paul does not pray for that. But such sense as we do have needs to be continually refocused, redirected, recentered in Christ so that "we may approve what is excellent" (1:10). The idea is that we become increasingly able to evaluate situations and put our weight on the side of what is really the best. It is that we have, in Moffatt's lovely translation, "a sense of what is vital."

I believe this prayer of Paul's needs desperately to be answered in our lives. Think of love without knowledge and discernment: where does it go, what does it mean, what does it do? It becomes sentiment, a good, warm feeling. It becomes emotion or affection without direction or subjection to the discipline and chastening of the Holy Spirit. Without such subjection, how quickly it can become lust! How quickly it can become ego-centered desire! How quickly it can identify with religious ecstasy and fervor! It can become passively tolerant of anybody and anything.

Consider the way the media portray ministers as innocuous, bland, tolerant, and spineless. It is a terrible distortion of both the gospel and the ministry, but it happens because the world knows only love without knowledge and discernment. Love must love what is worth loving, and that takes discrimination. Whatever "love, sweet love the world needs now," it is more than the good feelings of holding hands across the land and smiling at strangers and being tolerant of everyone else's point of view. The early church would have been outraged by such degradation of the burning love of the holy God manifested in Christ.

On the other hand, think of knowledge and discernment without love! Knowledge without love becomes destructive power—the extension of the ego, the tool and weapon of the self. The first temptation in the Garden of Eden was based on the desire for knowledge apart from love. The knowledge of good and evil—that is, the knowledge of everything—was the hook at the end of the serpent's line. The knowledge our first parents really needed was the knowledge of God, not of trees and fruit and good and evil!

Too often the hunger to know becomes the desire to master, and in mastery there is power. There is no pride like the pride of knowledge. I have read that the pride of intellect is such that its owner feels himself called to sit in the royal box, observing and judging the action of life—he is not "among the mimes who play the play." What he does not see is that he is indeed among the mimes who play the play, bound by his ego and blinded by his supposed intellectual integrity and aloof superiority. The world is dying of knowledge overload, without the discernment to weigh and make moral judgments. It has neither the motive nor the strength to choose the best. Knowledge without love produces technology without limits, ability without control. What fallen man can, he will do. Will we be able to control genetic engineering? Can we control our greed and save our environment? Have we ever *not* done something we knew how to do just because we knew it was not wise to do it? Not yet!

• Love Needs Wisdom—and Vice Versa

What shall we say about Christians? We desperately need the ability to make discerning moral judgments and the courage to make clear moral decisions. Why do Christian college students cheat on exams? Why is there so much divorce among us? Not all the children having children are children of the world—some are children of our churches. Shall Christians make decisions on their use of alcohol only on the basis of what advertisers have to say about "the good life"? Shall the attitudes of their friends make their decisions for them? Is a Christian's sexual behavior determined by the fear of AIDS?

These are serious issues. I am not talking about *what* decisions are finally made in any specific case; I am talking about *how* decisions are made and the kind of moral discernment that undergirds them. What Paul prays for is a kind of knowledge and discernment in the love of Christ that evaluates and makes decisions on the basis of what really is excellent and not what is prescribed by public opinion polls or the latest fads pushed by advertisers. Do we decide on issues such as world hunger or nuclear proliferation or abortion or genetic engineering or overpopulation on the basis of what we read in the papers or what some preacher says or whatever the group we belong to happens to think? The list is endless: the daily choices we make, the way we pay our debts or our taxes, the honesty and integrity of the work we do, how we relate to our families and neighbors.

Paul is praying, I believe, for a kind of perceptive knowledge and insight that will increasingly enable us to make real decisions on moral issues with intelligent and courageous love. It is a prayer for more clarity of thinking and more capacity for good practical judgment. Karl Barth quotes these lines:

> That small things should as small be seen,
> And great things great to us should seem.

This kind of love affects not only the moral decision-making processes, but our inner motivations also. Paul's phrase is "pure and blameless for the day of Christ" (1:10). The word translated "pure" refers in the New Testament to moral purity. "Blameless" means not stumbling or causing others to stumble, not causing harm to anyone. The idea of a pure inner life is found in several places in the letter to the Philippians: "Only let your manner of life be worthy of the gospel" (1:27); "Let each of you look not only to his own interests, but also to the interests of others" (2:4); "Do all things without grumbling or questioning, that you may be blameless and innocent, children of God without blemish in the midst of a crooked and perverse generation among whom you shine as lights in the world" (2:14–15).

It needs to be emphasized, however, that the inner sincerity and blamelessness of the Christians in this world are not necessarily obvious to the children of this world. They are words that express an inner relationship of openness and honesty before God. Paul does not pray that we will live in the world as perfect specimens of what God intended humanity to be. This would be the intolerable burden of an impossible goal. The view is toward the coming of the Lord, the day of Christ.

The Christian life is to be viewed in the light of that day's coming soon. This takes the inner life of the Christian out of the realm of achievement or accomplishment and puts it into a dynamic mode of hope and expectation. We are in process, we are on a journey of which Christ is both the way and the goal—and we are moving on. Paul's prayer does not call either the Philippians or us to the introspective examination of all the motives of our inner lives. It calls us to trust the divine initiative, to let love grow in wisdom, and to live sincerely and inoffensively in the light of the coming of Christ.

It is difficult for us not to take the lines of a prayer like this and try to make them work, one by one, in our lives. In that case, the shorter the prayer the better! In one sense, of course, that is precisely what we need to do. But how do such prayers keep from becoming lists of burdens to bear and duties to perform and changes to facilitate? For one thing, the presence now of the Christ who is to come produces in us a harvest of righteousness. It is not a struggle: we do not produce the fruit, he does. We immediately think of Galatians 5:22–23, which describes the fruit of the Spirit. We think also of Paul's words in Philippians 3:9: "not having a righteousness of my own, based on law, but that which is through faith in Christ, the righteousness of God that depends on faith." We know that the fruits of right living can only come as the fruit of right relationship with God in Christ. Whatever the fruits of righteousness are, they are such as only Christ can produce.

The very best thing about this wonderful prayer is that it directs the whole of our lives "to the glory and praise of God." We have talked about a fundamental shift in the center of gravity away from our self-preoccupation—even to be good and do good—to a concern for the glory of God. The initiative of God has begun the work; our lives, caught up in his purposes, produce the fruit of righteousness by Jesus Christ, all for the glory of God.

What a familiar, pious, ritualistic phrase: "to the glory and praise of God"! It sounds like a line in the third stanza of a Sunday morning hymn. But think a moment. In our world, glory—or its equivalent—is both the name and the goal of the game of life. And it is a deadly serious one. It is precisely what defines and controls the meaning of life. For desperate young people as for old ones, and for desperate warring nations, it is finally glory that determines who will live and who will die.

The truth is that Paul's familiar lines are not familiar at all. We have seen them, but we have not heard them. We have gone our own way, have sought by fair means or foul to achieve our own glory, our own praise—and have found our own destruction. Only a vision of the glory of God will save us from insipid love; only his praise will rescue us from egotistical knowledge. The glory and praise of God alone will clarify our vision of the righteousness that is in Christ and will produce in us its fruits.

We need a reminder before we leave the word study of this prayer. It was prayed for real people facing real problems, but it was prayed in confidence and joy because the One to whom it was prayed was himself working to answer it. That is a good word for us. Implicit in the prayer is the promise of the answer.

I remember a college freshman who was full of the love of the Lord and a desire to serve people. He would pray with a friend at two in the morning and miss his term exam later that day. He would fall in love with every girl who gave him a friendly smile. He had love without knowledge and without discernment. But this prayer of Paul has been—is being—answered in his life. The years have made a difference, for the grace of God has brought about in this man's life genuine discernment and wisdom. His Christian maturity is remarkable.

This very thing is going on in the church all the time. It is going on in ourselves. It may seem that we are "too soon old and too late smart," but it is not so. God is at work when it seems that nothing really worthwhile is happening in our lives. The fruits of righteousness are imperceptibly growing, and love is developing in knowledge and discernment even when we are not discerning it!

The Desert Fathers, who were led by God into the wilderness to worship and serve him in solitude, told their disciples that the best prayer is a simple prayer that is often repeated. A simple prayer, oft repeated, becomes the center of our daily meditation and so becomes a means of inner transformation. Such a prayer is this one that Paul prayed for the Philippians. It is a simple prayer which, oft repeated, can transform all the seasons of our lives.

My prayer for you is that you may have still more love—a love that is full of knowledge and every wise insight. I want you to be able to recognise the highest and the best, and to live sincere and blameless lives until the day of Christ. I want to see your lives full of true goodness, produced by the power that Jesus Christ gives you to the glory and praise of God (Phil. 1:9–11 PHILLIPS).

• Discussion Questions

1. In view of this prayer, what problems may have existed in the Philippian church?
2. How can we keep the balance between striving to be what God calls us to be and resting in his grace?
3. Obviously I'm reluctant to accept other Christians' attempts to give simple answers to life's problems. Do such answers bother you? Discuss.
4. How would you define the word *love* as it's used in the phrase "that your love may abound more and more" (1:9)?
5. Do you suppose that people who sponsor mass events in the name of brotherly love—such as rock concerts to raise money for world hunger—really believe that some good will come of it? What do you think?
6. Do you think Christians should strive to excel non-Christians in every arena of life? What are the advantages of such striving? the disadvantages?
7. How does Paul's prayer that we grow "with knowledge and all discernment" apply to people who have different educational backgrounds? different opinions about things?
8. I have emphasized the importance of exercising Christian love with knowledge and discernment. How would you illustrate this? Give an example of a Christian who has done this well. Now give an example of someone who has not done this (perhaps from your own experience).
9. I have used the word *glory* to refer to everything modern people strive to obtain. What other term(s) would you use to describe the object of our striving? How might this striving for "glory" be involved in the rising crime rate among well-to-do people as well as the poor? in the rise of teenage suicide? How might the trends of crime and suicide be affected if people devoted their lives to "the glory and praise of God"?

CHAPTER · 3

To Live Is Christ

I want you to know, brethren, that what has happened to me has really served to advance the gospel, so that it has become known throughout the whole praetorian guard and to all the rest that my imprisonment is for Christ; and most of the brethren have been made confident in the Lord because of my imprisonment, and are much more bold to speak the word of God without fear.

Some indeed preach Christ from envy and rivalry, but others from good will. The latter do it out of love, knowing that I am put here for the defense of the gospel; the former proclaim Christ out of partisanship, not sincerely but thinking to afflict me in my imprisonment. What then? Only that in every way, whether in pretense or in truth, Christ is proclaimed; and in that I rejoice. . . . it is my eager expectation and hope that I shall not be at all ashamed, but that with full courage now as always Christ will be honored in my body, whether by life or by death. For to me to live is Christ, and to die is gain (Phil. 1:12–18, 20–21).

● The key verse is the last one, familiar to us all: "For to me to live is Christ, and to die is gain." But I have a problem with it. It is too "spiritual." I cannot read it without saying yes. (How could any Christian say no?) Yet it floats on by me, not encountering me in a way that has any real meaning for my daily life. It is a good line for a hymn or the testimony of a mystic; and it is perfectly legitimate for an apostle like Paul to say it. But how in my busy world can I ever say such a thing?

But I am coming to the realization that the verse is not "spiritual" at all! The line just before it reads, "That with full courage now as always Christ will be honored in my body" (v. 20). Look at the line that follows: "If it is to be life in the flesh, that means fruitful labor for me" (v. 22). Sandwiched between the affirmation of bodily existence and the affirmation of plain hard work is this apparently mystical saying: "For me to live is Christ." How can it be?

Evidently Paul means something different from our usual "spiritual" interpetation. Verse 21 cannot be describing something that happens outside the realm of our here-and-now physical lives, for the words *body* (v. 20) and *flesh* (v. 22) anchor it to the present, physical world.

For Paul, it was the world of a prison compound, where the balance scales of life and death were tipped by hands other than his own. If he were allowed to live, it would mean he could keep on laboring for the Lord. He was ready to declare his commitment to the Lord in the present world. So when he says, "For me to live is Christ," he does not imply that he is ready to be taken away from the world and its concerns—though the world seemed gruesome at the moment he wrote these words. Paul was saying, rather, that the life he lived in the physical body was grounded in Christ, not in the physical circumstances of the body itself.

• Advancing the Gospel

If we begin reading at verse 12, we discover that our key verse concludes three significant sayings. Here is the first: "I want you to know, brethren, that what has happened to me has really served to advance the gospel" (1:12). Something mattered more to Paul than all the heartache that he had experienced—it was the advancement of the gospel of Jesus Christ. Remember what had happened to Paul. Several years earlier, he had taken some bad advice (from some good men!) and had gotten into a lot of trouble in Jerusalem. A simple, pious act of paying temple expenses for some fellow

32

Jews had been misunderstood; some supposed them to be Gentiles—and a riot exploded. A Roman tribune took him into protective custody, then transferred him to Caesarea. Unable to get a fair hearing there, he appealed to be heard by the emperor. Eventually, he found himself sitting in a prison compound in Rome, awaiting his day in court (Acts 21:17–28:31).

But regard Paul's words: "What has happened to me has really served to advance the gospel."

Please understand—I don't believe that everything that happens to us Christians is somehow related to the gospel. Nor do I believe that everything that comes to us, no matter how evil or undeserved, is somehow made useful for the kingdom of God. But I believe Paul's words give us a point of reference, other than ourselves, that helps us endure the grievous things that happen to us. In Paul's own case, the gospel of Christ was advanced by the unfair circumstances of his arrest and imprisonment. That sort of thing may happen in our lives as well. In every case, something matters more than how we are affected by the events of our lives—and that "something" is the advancement of the gospel.

I was visiting in the home of a pastor who told me about various burdens and troubles that his congregation was laying on his tired shoulders. We were sitting at lunch when his phone rang. He listened to the message, said a few words, and walked back to the table. He sat down with a heavy sigh. One of his people had become suddenly ill and had been rushed to a local hospital. "On top of everything else, now this," he groaned. "She's sick in the hospital, and I've got to visit her! Don't these people know I have enough to do already?"

I was thinking, *Brother, maybe you need to find another church—or another vocation. I don't think you will be able to do this much longer!* He had nothing to say about the trauma of her sudden illness; he uttered no word of pastoral concern; he did not want to discuss how he might minister to the patient or her family. But, worse, he voiced no concern about how this crisis might advance the gospel.

I'm sure the burdens of his pastorate were real. He was worn out and weighed down with cares. And I could see that the cares of his people genuinely affected him. But for that evening, at least, he lost touch with what really mattered—the advancement of the gospel. Does this ever happen with you?

• Proclaiming Christ

The second saying probes our conscience a bit deeper. Paul explains that some Christians were made bold by his bondage, so that they began to preach the gospel more effectively and began to show an intensified loyalty to the apostle and his Lord. But others were making a different response to his situation. As long as Paul had been actively in charge, they had little opportunity to assert themselves; but now that he is set aside, they see their moment had arrived. They are ready to take over. They are preaching "from envy and rivalry" with Paul (v. 15). So Paul says: "What then? Only that in every way, whether in pretense or truth, Christ is proclaimed; and in that I rejoice" (v. 18).

These words disturb me. They bring up the painful subject of motive in the ministry. How does one discern a minister's rivalry or goodwill, partisanship or love, pretense or truth?

I am not the only person who questions the motives of those who preach the gospel. What is behind the incredible merchandising of the gospel on television and radio? Why do big-name Christian singers and speakers command such large fees and indulge themselves in luxury? What is behind the hype for their records and tapes (not books, of course)? How do the masters of multimillion-dollar ministry empires manage to explain their moral indiscretions, while preaching the judgment of God on the sins of our materialistic society? How far will they go to court the favor of their audience? What will be the limits of their ludicrous fund-raising efforts? Must the gospel be smothered in theatrics and commercialism and lights and mikes and background tapes?

But one time at a retreat for pastors' wives, my wife and I met a beautiful woman who was involved with her husband in leading a lively, growing church. We learned that she had been converted while watching one of the show-biz Christian programs that I keep turning off (so that I can remain converted). The Lord said to me, *Well, Reuben, who made you the judge?*

The problem is far from settled in my own mind. But one thing is clear: I am not the judge. Paul's point is that he learned that what matters is not *his* evaluation of the motives of those who preach the gospel. Motives matter and methods matter—they matter very much—but what really matters is the preaching of Christ.

The pastor's wife saw Christ through all the glitter of that television program, and she was totally unaware of the trappings that were so offensive to me!

Every congregation of believers is obliged to judge the teachings of its ministers. I sense in today's evangelical world a tragic loss of discernment. I wonder to what extent a culturally conditioned church is responsible for the shallow preaching of its ego-centered ministry. When will the people of God call their leaders to account for their selfish methods of management and their materialistic lifestyles?

But I have a deeper struggle with my own motives. Do I ever act with totally pure motives? I suspect that everyone's motives are mixed; my concern is what my motives are mixed with. If they are mixed with repentance and openness to the illumination and cleansing judgment of the Holy Spirit, then my motives may be progressively centered in Christ.

We cannot be deaf to Paul's concern in this passage. He wants to be sure that Christ is preached, regardless of the mixture of motives in his friends—or in his enemies! Are we willing to subvert all of our personal criticisms and reservations to that end?

• Honoring Christ

The third saying brings us closer to our theme text: "It is my eager expectation and hope that I shall not be at all ashamed, but that with full courage now as always Christ will be honored in my body, whether by life or by death" (1:20). Paul wants to be sure, regardless of what happens to him, that the gospel of Jesus Christ is advanced. And he wants to be sure, whether he lives or dies, that he will honor Christ.

Let us not overspiritualize that statement. The climax of Paul's series of declarations is a *bodily life* in which Christ is honored. Paul talks of honoring Christ through his hands and feet, his brain and lips. He longs to honor the Lord if his physical life continues or if it is ended.

Can we sense the peril of Paul's situation? His words reveal his uncertainty and ambivalence about the future. Beyond his own feelings and expectations, however, one overriding concern sustains him from day to day: He will do whatever he can to bring glory to Christ.

● Keeping Christ at the Center

"For me to live is Christ, and to die is gain" (1:21). What a declaration! It does not mean that Paul lived in a kind of mystical detachment from the real world of bodily experience. He struggled and suffered and cared for the churches that he had established. He wrote letters to them, traveled to visit them, and made tents to pay for his expenses. He did not think about Christ all the time. He was that much like us.

I believe that his phrase "to live is Christ" meant for Paul that Christ was the central focus of all that he did. Everything in his life obtained value in relation to Jesus and the advancement of the gospel. Christ gave such meaning, purpose, significance, and cohesiveness to Paul's life and life's work that even if he died, who he was and what he was as an apostle would not be lost. Rather, his purpose would be secured forever. Paul's life could never be rendered useless because it was centered in the Lord.

Perhaps it is be helpful to ask, How would you complete the sentence "To me to live is _____ "? At this point, it is not enough to write "Christ" and quit thinking. I want you to realize that is not an easy sentence to complete. What gives meaning, value, and cohesiveness to your life? What is your life center?

My wife and I know some people who would have to write *Shaklee* or *Amway* in that blank. Perhaps the name of your company belongs there.

Tennis, anyone? How about baseball or football? For many people, sports is the very meaning of life. A sportscaster in our town loves to make people angry by saying, right in the middle of a season, "It's only a game!" Some Christians have to make a tough decision when a play-off game is scheduled at the same time as a church service. Is it only a game?

What would you write in the blank? A relationship? Your spouse or your children? Your hobby? Your job? Your status or place in the community? Your achievement of success? Money? (Shall we think about the lives and homes that have been destroyed for the sake of success and money?)

For some people, the meaning of life is "being right." All of us know persons who cannot bear to be wrong, persons who will move heaven and earth to prove themselves right.

Perhaps you should write "my ministry" in the blank. (*Ministry*—what a wonderful word! What word did we use before we started calling everything we do our *ministry?*) Should the name of your Sunday school class, Bible study group, or church go in the blank? Or should it be the name of some other service activity you enjoy, because of the power and influence it brings?

Honestly, what are you living for? Does it have anything to do with the gospel of Jesus Christ?

Then what would it be to die? Paul said, "To me, to live is Christ and to die is gain." How would you complete that sentence? There are two good reasons to think about this side of it.

One of them is that we are going to die. Some years ago, my father died. I wondered at the time, *How could anyone so strong and dependable ever die?* Then my mother died. When your father and mother are both gone, it is not difficult to realize that your own generation is the next to go. But it is hard to accept the fact of your own inevitable death.

The second reason is that much of our self-defeating behavior comes from the fact that the things or persons that give meaning to our lives will be gone someday. We can deny the inevitability of that. We can withdraw from the real world and build a fantasy kingdom—a place where we impute permanence to what is transitory, deify what is not divine, and confer worth upon what is not worthy. But it is all a fiction. Our false values may deceive us for a time. They may sanction a frenzied effort to hold onto what we have, denying the ultimate reality of death and decay. But, sooner or later, the truth comes crashing in around us.

I remember reading about a group of people who built an enormous sand castle on a beach in Florida. They used 48,000 tons of sand and built it fifty-two feet high. We might say, "What a foolish waste! No matter how intricate the artistry or how ingenious the construction, it's destined to go out with the next tide! Nothing will be left but a few photographs and a column of newsprint." But the builders may not have been so foolish after all; they did it for the fun of the doing, with no false expectation of the permanence of their work. Perhaps there is more moral integrity in sand-castle building than in building our little personal empires that are as easily dissolved, but which are built with the illusion of permanence.

Some of us are building sand castles with our lives, while denying the transient character of our constructions. We will forfeit a marriage for a temporary affair. We will sacrifice a lifetime of business integrity for a fleeting financial victory. We will give up the values that we say we treasure most to obtain more money and power.

Consider the way our popular love songs impute to the lover qualities that can be found only in God. We say that a lover gives our lives meaning and value and joy. We say the lover brings us happiness and fulfillment. The object of our affection is adored, longed for, and worshiped. I'm not convinced that the bored night-club frequenters who listen to these words sung by thrice-divorced entertainers really believe what they hear. But tragically, they have no one in their lives to fulfill the profound longings expressed in the lyrics. When people entrust their lives to other gods, other goals, and other loves besides Christ, they cast their lot with the false gods' own vulnerability to death. The false gods exact their toll. The tragedy of despair is awesome.

Would it be all right to die? Of course not! It would be all right with me to die, I suppose. The children are grown, and Mary Jo would have a lot more money than she ever will while I'm alive.

But of course it would not be all right to die. What comes to mind when you read that awful question? *I can't die now. I want to . . . I need to . . . I've got to . . . It would mean they would have to . . . .* What if you could bring all those reasons to Jesus and leave them at the foot of his cross? That's not an escape from responsible living. It is the way to freedom. The only way to guarantee the permanence of our values is to center them in Jesus. "All other ground is sinking sand."

If Jesus is at the center of life, things can be what they really are. They can assume their appropriate meaning and value. We don't have to put the weight of our trust on things that cannot bear it. Our play can be play; our work can be work; our prayer can be prayer; and our worship can be worship. Life can be what God meant it to be, in all its sacred seriousness and trivial gaiety.

Sports can become our recreation.

Success in business can be simply that.

Our relationships can become what they ought to be.

We can be free from the lordship of things, activities, and other people because our meaning and fulfillment are not found in a deceitful, dying world structure. When Jesus is the center of our lives, false dependencies will be illuminated and displaced. Destructive ties can be seen for what they really are—and abandoned. When we find life's meaning in the service of Jesus Christ, we will stop seeking everywhere else what can be found only in him.

If life is Christ, then even death can be what it really is. We do not have to cover it with flowers and kind sayings and songs about beautiful isles somewhere. We do not have to pretend that death is a gentle friend; nor do we have to see it as our terrible enemy. We must not deny the reality of death. But foremost in our thinking is the fact that Christ is our life; and in him, death is gain.

The Holy Spirit is calling us to a new way of perceiving reality, in which the ultimate reality is Christ. When he is at the center of life—when life means living in Christ—we are "at home" with our present situation. When our ultimate purpose is to promote the gospel of Christ, our identity will not be lost when we die, because we find our identity in him.

● **Discussion Questions**

1. "For me to live is Christ," Paul says (v. 21). Do you think it is difficult to apply this verse to everyday living? Why or why not?

2. Do you agree that much of what happens to us has little to do with the gospel? Compare Philippians 1:12 with Romans 8:28. Do these verses mean that God uses *everything* that happens in our lives to accomplish something good?

3. Explain how an unexpected event in your life (such as a serious illness or the loss of a job) might further the cause of the gospel. In Paul's case, something totally unfair and unjust (his imprisonment) was used for God's glory. Is this often the case when God's people are treated unjustly?

4. I am obviously troubled by what appear to be the selfish and mercenary motives of some singers and speakers who are dominating the evangelical scene. Do you think my concern is legitimate or exaggerated? Explain.

5. Distinguish between "performance" and worship in church services. Do you think worship style is simply a matter of taste, or are there spiritual hazards in it?

6. The Bible says we are not to judge the motives of those who preach, but we are to judge their message. Can we really separate the two? If so, how?

7. We may be quick to identify in other people the bad motives that we find in ourselves, especially if we wish to draw attention away from our own motives. Does this help to explain our response to hype and glitz of some evangelists? Discuss.

8. What are some ways that Christ might be honored by a person's death? (Remember that Paul was not an old saint who died peacefully in his sleep, with his family and friends nearby.)

9. Complete the sentence: "For me to live is _____." Do you find my criticisms in this section too harsh? Why or why not?
10. I said that we seek life's meaning in things that will be destroyed by death. What examples would you give?
11. Discuss this statement: *If Christ is at the center, life can be what it truly is.* Apply this to your own life.

CHAPTER · 4

Life Worthy
of the Gospel

Only let your manner of life be worthy of the gospel of Christ, so that whether I come and see you or am absent, I may hear of you that you stand firm in one spirit, with one mind striving side by side for the faith of the gospel, and not frightened in anything by your opponents. This is a clear omen to them of their destruction, but of your salvation, and that from God. For it has been granted to you that for the sake of Christ you should not only believe in him but also suffer for his sake, engaged in the same conflict which you saw and now hear to be mine (Phil. 1:27–30).

● Philippians 1:21 ("For me to live is Christ . . . ") is a stirring affirmation, but it is obviously not the climax of Paul's letter. It comes early in the letter and reflects a Christ-centeredness that runs as a constant theme throughout the rest. In Christ, Paul says, death is surely gain. But until then, life goes on. So the apostle challenges us to a "manner of life" that is "worthy of the gospel." Once again, we see a shift in the center of gravity away from our own concerns to God and the gospel of his Son, Jesus Christ.

Who lives worthy of the gospel? How can anyone ever be worthy?

At the outset, we must say that only Jesus Christ is worthy. Anytime the word *worthy* is used in connection with us, it must denote something of our relationship to him. Never can it be understood to refer to something we have achieved or earned by ourselves.

I am glad that Paul's statement is an exhortation, not a command. But it is a serious exhortation. Placed before us are a vision and a calling that demand all we have to give.

• Seek Relationship With Christ

We saw in the first chapter that the *gospel* is the good news of God's coming in Jesus to redeem, to save, to reconcile, and to heal us. A life worthy of the gospel must flow out of the gospel itself. It cannot come from any system or program that merely promotes the gospel.

Paul knew about such systems. Later in this epistle, we learn about his background in Pharisaism. He describes the radical transition in his life when he moved from dependence upon the system to a personal relationship with Jesus Christ. But the early church still struggled with this tendency to rely on a religious system, and so do we.

In this regard, we should pay careful attention to the experience of the Jews in Old Testament times. In response to God's initiative, the Israelites became the covenant people of God. Their covenant relationship with him was lived, on the one hand, in rituals of worship and, on the other, in the lifestyle of the Ten Commandments and the Book of the Covenant. The divine-human relationship was expressed in their unique ways of worshiping and living. Eventually, these unique ways became codified and systematized. For the first generation under this covenant, the system genuinely expressed their relationship with God—first came the relationship, then the system. But for later generations, the system came first, then the relationship; and when system dominates, relationship grows cold. The first Christians were not immune to this syndrome.

Paul speaks to this point when he insists that a Christian's life must be related primarily to Jesus Christ, not to the religious system that promotes the message about him. The Jews in the congregation at Philippi struggled to understand the relationship between the tradition of Judaism and their new life in Christ; the Gentiles struggled to understand the relationship between their proud Greek or Roman traditions and the new lifestyle demands of Jesus' gospel. Yet their struggles could not be resolved by an ingenious system. Only a personal relationship with Christ himself could hold these tensions in creative bond.

It's so easy to identify our adherence to the system with our life in the gospel. It's easy to assume that our conformity to church tradition is essential to the Christian life. But we perpetuate the confusion of legalism when we do this—when we affirm the spiritual integrity of Christians who conform to our system and exclude those who don't seem to fit. How many of us judge ourselves and others on the basis of conformity to the church's traditional way of doing things or on the basis of the current "Christian" position on a given moral issue? It is time for us to hear the apostle Paul again. We must remember that the religious system isn't our standard. The gospel is!

• Understand God's Personal Word

A life worthy of the gospel of Jesus Christ must be defined by that gospel, not by any person who proclaims it. Notice how many times in this short epistle Paul refers to his presence or absence with regard to the church at Philippi. He seems very uncertain about his future. He might live and return to them, or he might die and not see them again (1:19–26). He might come to them again, or he might be absent for the rest of his life (1:27). He intends to visit the Philippians again, but he is not sure how the trial will go with him (2:19–24). In any case, he says, his presence is not significant to the welfare of the Philippian church; their lives are conditioned not by him or by any other evangelist, but by the gospel itself.

We modern Christians seems to have an inordinate hunger for some teacher with charisma to tell us what is right to do and what we ought to believe and how we should perceive the Christian faith or the Christian position on this or that issue. I am amazed at the numbers of Christians who pay high fees for seminars at which they learn how to understand the Bible, how to communicate with one another, how to discipline their children, or how to be effective leaders and thus fulfill their ministries in the church.

What one leader says or how another teacher explains the biblical message can be the Holy Spirit's means of life-changing insight. I don't disparage the need for good teachers. But my concern is that we are prone to interpret the Christian faith solely in terms that are structured for us by someone else's perceptions. We can easily define "life worthy of the gospel" by someone else's principles or guidelines or helpful hints—and not by the gospel.

Who portrays the worthy Christian life for you? Against whom do you judge yourself or the Christians around you? Who defines your Christian perception of reality, your Christian "worldview"? We should thank God for every leader and teacher of spiritual insight. But Jesus, whose Spirit is the Spirit of truth, is to be our guide.

If I could give you one precious gift, it would be the ability to trust your own mind and heart to understand God's guidance for you. You must begin following the guidance of God in your own life as you seek to live in the light of the gospel. A life worthy of the gospel lays upon you the wonderful, releasing burden of living from the inside out. It lays upon you the liberating yoke of the responsibility to think, act, and obey the Spirit of God for yourself.

• Live in the New Covenant Community

From this text, I also understand the life worthy of the gospel to be a life in community. This life together enables us to trust the leading of the Holy Spirit for ourselves. If we are left to follow our private inclinations, we would only isolate ourselves from others— and ultimately destroy ourselves. But our membership in the body of believers provides both the arena of our freedom and the context of our accountability.

Paul's phrase "manner of life" (1:27) is a translation of a Greek word from which we get the English term *politics*. It refers to life as a group of citizens. He indicates that life worthy of the gospel is the Christian's citizen life in the new covenant community. In Philippians 3:20, Paul uses a related word when he says, "Our *commonwealth* is in heaven. . . . "

Do we know that we are covenantally bound together, as surely as God has bound himself to us? When God called the Israelites to himself and entered a covenantal relationship with them, their quality of life was to be defined by their relationship with that covenant community. Their relationships with one another were not to be based on the practices of neighboring cultures or even on their former tribal connections. They were to begin dealing with one another as fellow members of a new covenant community under God.

In the early days, the Israelites had no king; their ties were not economic or political. They did not always get along well with one another; but they were bound together by their covenant with God. In times of war or trouble, they responded to protect the community because the call of God's covenant was upon them.

A profoundly significant change took place when they began to be ruled by kings. They forgot the politics of covenant love and learned the politics of money and power. Archaeological digs have shown that at the time of Elijah (ca. 850 B.C.) most of the Israelite houses were of the same general quality. About one hundred years later, during the time of Amos and Hosea, the Israelite towns had shacks and hovels at one end, but luxurious housing at the other. It was no longer a community of brother and brother, family and family; it was a society of master and slave, owner and tenant, creditor and debtor.

The scathing judgment messages of Amos were directed to the Israelites' loss of covenant relationship. That loss allowed the rich to exploit the poor. They forgot their covenant in the competitive economic marketplace. The rich got richer, the poor got poorer, and the judgment of God destroyed their affluent nation.

We cannot avoid the question, How do we Christians relate to other people? We cannot live as though the economic and political structures of this world did not exist. But, as Christians, our fundamental posture toward others must not be based on the ego-centered, profit-motivated patterns of secular society. We belong to the community of the New Covenant, and the way we live is to be worthy of the gospel that calls us into being under God.

I remember a time when the president of our college was terminally ill. I was the college chaplain, and I often visited him in his home. One day, on my way back from a visit there, I met a colleague who asked me how the president was doing. He said, "You know, I feel guilty that I haven't been over to see him. But, after all, he is the president. I don't know if it would be all right for me to visit him."

Can you see what I saw in that conversation? A Christian brother was sick and dying; another Christian brother was interested and caring. But a great invisible wall had been erected between the one who hurt and the one who cared—an artificial, arbitrary barrier that divided the president from his staff, the corporate head from middle management—and thus effectively separated two brothers in the Lord.

The Lord would not have this sort of thing among us.

I know no easy way to break down the social, economic, and political structures that divide us. These structures, which have been incorporated into the life of the church, exercise a destructive power. For example, what happens when the pastor becomes the corporate head and the staff become middle management? I do not deny that we need structure, leadership, and authority in any kind of society—including the church. But what happens when we relate to one another in terms of our roles, positions, or titles, rather than as brothers and sisters in the Lord?

It is difficult to know how to relate covenantally to one another in today's culture. Can a Christian take profit from another's loss? Should we, for the sake of church policy, destroy a brother or sister for whom Christ died? The list of questions is endless. I can ask them only because I share in the guilt and stand in need of forgiveness for the extent to which I have forsaken my covenant bonds and used other people for money, status, and power. It is as true of me as of old Israel—my relationships with others express my relationship with God. In the words of Paul, I hear the word of God that calls us back to covenant relationships. Only in such brotherly and sisterly fellowship can justice be done and peace prevail in the community of faith.

● Strive for Oneness in Christ

When Paul challenges me to live "worthy of the gospel," I expect him to deliver some word of ethical teaching or a directive toward moral righteousness and love. What I read instead is this: "That you stand firm in one spirit, with one mind striving side by side for the faith of the gospel, and not frightened in anything by your opponents" (1:27b–28). "One spirit," "one mind," "side by side"—perhaps these phrases can help us understand the word *worthy* a little better.

If living a life "worthy of the gospel" means having perfect inner motives and exhibiting flawless outward behavior, the gospel is reduced to nothing more than an exhortation to moral striving and ethical struggle, and it can never free us from the sense of perpetual failure. How many Christians live with continual guilt because they don't quite measure up to being "worthy" in this sense of the word? They never quite meet the standards or expectations imposed by themselves or others. How many Christians have said, "I can never be worthy," and have abandoned their faith?

A lady in a church I served in Honolulu used to say to me at the door of the sanctuary, "Reverend, I'm just an apprentice Christian. When I get good enough, I will be a real one." She never was quite "worthy"—and, like all the rest of us, never will be!

But what if a life "worthy of the gospel" means being of one mind and spirit with other Christians, working side by side with them? Such a life must not depend upon our own moral achievements. It must involve failure as well as success and weakness as well as strength. It must be the kind of life where interdependence is valued, rather than avoided. I believe we have not begun to comprehend the full significance of our oneness in Christ.

Paul's words to the Philippians reveal his concern about the possible fragmentation of the Christian fellowship. In chapter 2 he urges them to be of the "same mind," the "same love," living in "full accord," and acting with "one mind." He exhorts them to "do nothing from selfishness or conceit" (2:3) and to follow the self-emptying example of Jesus. He pleads with Euodia and Syntyche "to agree in the Lord" (4:2).

The apostle would have been appalled if he could have seen the divisions that fracture the community of believers today. We ourselves are overwhelmed as we reflect on the sickly witness of the divided body of Christ in our world.

We recently witnessed the news media's publicizing a "holy war" among the leaders of the American religious television empires. What will be the results of such ego conflicts? Yet this is only one illustration of the divisions among Christians.

Are we seeking to be "worthy of the gospel" in the wrong ways? Real worthiness is not found in our denominational strength or doctrinal purity or shared spiritual experiences; nor is it found in our personal purity or moral achievements. It is found in our common purpose and our common love, expressed in our side-by-side labor for the gospel of Christ.

• Trust the Power of the Gospel

The gospel addresses many great causes and great needs in our world. The social problems of our generation are of awesome magnitude. World hunger, overpopulation, social injustice, poverty, disease, and growing crime rates are just a few of them. Yet the gospel speaks to all of these problems. It declares that God has come in Jesus to destroy the works of the Devil (see 1 John 3:8). He has called us to participate in his saving purposes. Some people would identify those saving purposes with their particular cause, and they invite me to join their crusade. But we weaken the message of the gospel when we define it in terms of our own personal campaigns.

Paul reminds us that we are to fight for the full faith of the gospel. We must let the gospel of Christ speak its word of judgment and healing, both to us and to the unsaved world. But we must not identify the gospel with our own causes or concerns.

We can trust the power of the gospel to change the sinful, self-destructive patterns of our society. Only in the gospel do we find power to heal the wounds and cleanse the infections of our world. We can take up various causes and "work while it is yet day" to find victory in these causes, recognizing that we will differ on many things and that the road ahead will be difficult. All the more, then we must learn to stand together "in one spirit and one mind, working side by side"!

Our oneness in the struggle for the faith of the gospel is an omen of the eventual destruction of the forces we oppose. This declaration of the apostle, taken seriously, is a strong word of hope as we live in the presence of our "opponents." Our side-by-side striving for the faith of the gospel is the sign that the dark forces of the enemy will ultimately be destroyed.

The truth is that one by one, group by group, we aren't much. Let's set a revolving pedestal in front of the church and take turns standing on it in the presence of the congregation. Let's look each other over. We would see some wonderful and beautiful things about each other—but mostly we are religious organizations of the human, flawed type. Put us side by side with one mind and spirit, striving together for the faith of the gospel, and we are invincible.

We are engaged in a battle with the sinful forces of this world. But the battle is the Lord's. And that battle has already been won through the death and resurrection of our Lord Jesus. Our real battle is not with the sinful powers of this world, but with ourselves.

Remember these words of the apostle: "I am sure that he who began a good work in you will bring it to completion at the day of Jesus Christ" (1:6). That is our hope in the conflict. We believe and we suffer, but we are not frightened. Side by side with Christ, we are invincible!

• Discussion Questions

1. The word *gospel* is crucial to understanding this chapter. How do you define it?
2. It is difficult—perhaps impossible—to separate our understanding of the gospel from the church or the group in which we heard it. Why does this make Bible study so important?
3. How do persons who have grown up in the church come to know Christ in a different way from those who meet him on the "outside"?
4. I am concerned that so many of us depend on the teachings of influential Christian teachers. Do you share this concern? Why or why not?
5. I said that I would like to give you the ability to trust your own mind and heart in discerning God's guidance. How do you respond to that statement? How does the church fellowship provide some "checks and balances" to prevent us from acting on the basis of selfish inclinations?
6. Give an example of how a Christian could relate to someone "covenantally," in contrast to dealing with that person according to role or status?
7. Can Christians follow two standards—"business is business" in the world and "love one another" in the church? For example, do you think a Christian should be able to profit from someone else's bankruptcy or foreclosure? Discuss.
8. I believe we should not define life "worthy of the gospel" in terms of moral purity or superior ethical standards, but in terms of our oneness with other Christians. Do you agree? Discuss.
9. I do not think it is possible (perhaps not even desirable) to do away with denominations. If we keep the denominational structure, what are some practical ways in which we can strive together, side by side with other Christians?

10. The "striving" that Paul describes is not striving for a particular social cause, but "for the faith of the gospel." What issues enlist the striving of Christians today? Give examples of what it means for Christians to strive "for the faith of the gospel" today.

C H A P T E R · 5

The Mind of Christ

So if there is any encouragement in Christ, any incentive of love, any participation in the Spirit, any affection and sympathy, complete my joy by being of the same mind, having the same love, being in full accord and of one mind. Do nothing from selfishness or conceit, but in humility count others better than yourselves. Let each of you look not only to his own interests, but also to the interests of others. Have this mind among yourselves, which is yours in Christ Jesus, who, though he was in the form of God, did not count equality with God a thing to be grasped, but emptied himself, taking the form of a servant, being born in the likeness of men. And being found in human form he humbled himself and became obedient unto death, even death on a cross. Therefore God has highly exalted him and bestowed on him the name which is above every name, that at the name of Jesus every knee should bow, in heaven and on earth and under the earth, and every tongue confess that Jesus Christ is Lord, to the glory of God the Father (Phil. 2:1–11).

● This marvelous hymn of praise to the Son of God is doubtless one of the best-known and most profound of all Paul's writings. But it does not arise out of Paul's contemplation of the incarnation of Christ. Rather, it comes out of his deep concern for the unity of the Philippian church. Usually, we think of this epistle as one of hopefulness and joy. But we must also note that the apostle is troubled by the divisions—real and potential—within the Philippian fellowship. Paul appeals to the Philippians to live in "full accord" and with "one mind." He appeals to the moving power of their relationship to Christ.

This is a radical summons that is based on the strength of the Philippians' fellowship with Christ and with one another. Listen to Paul's entreaty:

> If your relationship to Christ has any power to influence you or counsel you; if your union with Christ can make any appeal to you; if love has any persuasive power to move you or open you toward one another; if we are sharers together in the Spirit; if your hearts have any tenderness or sympathy. . . .

Clearly, Paul believes that the Philippians have these desires. He is confident of making an appeal for unity because of these commitments.

But his appeal is not to their logic. The call is going to be for radical reversal in their mindset, a "U-turn" of the mind. Such reversal does not come only through a change of intellectual perspective, but through the concurrence of mind and emotions in a way that gets the whole person involved.

What determines your thinking as a Christian? Does your relationship with Christ influence all of your decisions? Are you sensitive to the gentle nudging of his presence in your life? Does his love guide the way you view the world and the way you deal with other people?

Does it mean anything to you to be one in the Spirit with other Christians, sharing a common life in Christ? Does that common life determine how you act toward others in the body? Do you have Christian tenderness and sympathy in your heart—and do those attitudes affect your behavior in any way?

These were the questions that Paul put to the Philippians. We should feel the full force of them as well.

● "Complete My Joy"

The only clear command in the passage is, "Complete my joy" (v. 2). That hardly seems to be a legitimate command—"Do this to make me happy." But Fred Craddock makes the point that Paul was so deeply identified with Christ (1:8) and with the church (1:7) that his joy was not his alone. It was shared with them in the love of Christ. The completion of Paul's joy was the oneness and harmony of the church at Philippi.

We are tempted to say, "Paul, how naive can you be?" We assume that Jews and Gentiles worshiped in the same congregation. Lydia the businesswoman was there; no doubt the ex-jailer was, too. Euodia and Syntyche were evidently strong personalities in the church. Also present were Clement, Epaphroditus, and various people in the service of Emperor Nero. Think about their various backgrounds. Imagine this congregation meeting together for worship and service. Now say to them, "Same mind . . . same love . . . full accord . . . that's how it must be!" Impossible!

The pluralism among modern Christians is, if anything, more pronounced. My own experience in a Christian liberal arts college underscores this. How are faculty members in the science department to think like those in the humanities? How can physical education majors think like art majors? Our whole educational system assumes diverse ways of thinking and different approaches to problems. Yet the members of these diverse disciplines are supposed to worship and serve together in a local congregation.

Within your own congregation I'm sure there are differences of gifts, ministries, and ways of thinking. How can Paul's words be taken seriously, considering the different ways people think and act in the real world of the church today?

● Same Mind, Same Soul

Having the "same mind" (v. 2) does not mean being in agreement on all things. It means having the same mind-set, looking at things from the same orientation or point of view. This Christian point of view is not one that we happen to be born with; it is ours as a result of our being in Christ Jesus and learning to see things from his point of view. We can have the same mind as other

Christians because we have the same love—the love of Christ. As someone said, "The Christ in me will not fight with the Christ in you."

"Full accord" (v. 2) means literally to have the "same soul." We Christians are soul brothers and soul sisters, people whose inner lives are joined in harmony and full accord. We have a oneness of inner spirit that comes from our oneness in Christ and our sharing of his life.

Paul's final, repeated call for being of "one mind" (v. 2) expresses the intensity of Paul's concern. He urgently desires that the Christian fellowship have unity and integrity in the way they understand the world around them.

We do not know what specific problems in the Philippian church lay behind the apostle's call for unity. In chapter 1 he mentioned those who preached from envy and rivalry. Paul's own imprisonment had led to that problem. He mentioned two women who may have been competing for leadership within the church (4:2). Whatever the problem, Paul stressed that the Philippians were to have the same mind-set or point of view; they were to share the same love and have harmony of soul. Their hearts should beat together with the same purpose—to bring glory to God in the service of Jesus Christ.

I fear that Paul's words may seem so radical that we will dismiss them as inapplicable to our situation. We are tempted to leave them unexamined and unauthoritative, assuming they have no discernible impact on our lives.

Worse, we may think this is merely a bland request for more kindness and harmony among Christians. We may suppose that Paul is encouraging us to try a little harder to be nice to each other, endeavoring to maintain a spirit of unity in our church meetings.

Either of these assumptions would lose the cutting power of what Paul says. If we dismiss what Paul says—regardless of our reasons—we continue to wallow in false perceptions, destructive attitudes, and divisive behaviors.

Can the admonitions of Paul have a direct bearing on our

pluralistic Christian community today? Can we really have one mind and one heart? I believe the answer is found in these words:

> Do nothing from selfishness or conceit, but in humility count others better than yourselves. Let each of you look not only to his own interests, but also to the interests of others (2:3–4).

Our closed ways of thinking destructively divide us. We suffer from "hardening of the categories" and selfish pride.

Our doctrines, beliefs, and convictions—even when rightly held—must not be tightly held. They must be lovingly affirmed with the compassion of Christ and in the profound awareness of our oneness with other Christians. So many "right" things divide us from one another in the body of Christ: how we understand the birth of Jesus, the way we interpret his miracles and teachings, how we perceive the meaning of his death and resurrection, how we view the Bible as the inspired Word of God, what we believe about the sacraments, and so on. We do not agree on these fundamental beliefs. Yet our nonagreement does not really divide us; our hardened ways of thinking do.

We hold our beliefs in sanctioned terms. We perceive any difference of vocabulary or point of view as a compromise of orthodoxy. I think this is why Paul repeatedly emphasized that we should exercise love in our dealings with other Christians.

No one could accuse Paul of being indifferent about doctrine. But a close look at this epistle reveals that Paul had an intense concern for the personal dimension of Christian teaching. His prayer for the Philippians arises from a heart filled with affection (1:8–9). He can tolerate even misguided preaching if it does not disrupt the unity of the church (1:15–18). And he believes the clearest sign of the church's ultimate victory is Christians' ability to work side by side, despite their differences (1:27–30).

Our categories of truth/doctrine must ultimately bow before the Person who said, "I am the way, and the truth, and the life" (John 14:6). Will we ever listen to the exhortation of Christ? Will we ever let love and compassion melt our stiffened structures and learn to think together? Will we ever recognize the Spirit in others as well as ourselves and find in one another soul brothers and sisters?

● The Danger of Pride

We are divided from other Christians because love has not been our dominating force; our egos and pride have gotten the upper hand. Threats to our doctrines do not separate us as much as threats to our egos. We defend challenged territory more than challenged beliefs. The kind of humility Paul proposes in verses 3–4 is alien to our self-centered, autonomous world. It certainly is not going to originate with us!

Perhaps you have attended a church committee meeting where the discussion was vigorous and where opposing views were strongly—even hotly—debated. At some point, a certain position was stoutly defended and someone's feelings got hurt. The victim's feelings were so identified with a position that contrary opinions were taken personally. Sudden, paralyzing fear seized the meeting. After that exchange, everyone in the group proceeded with great caution, skirting the real issues and backing away from creative possibilities. The group's goal shifted from solving the church's problems to appeasing a person's ego and keeping the peace. The group may have eventually decided to rescind its action, but there was no soul harmony in the meeting, no unity of mind and heart.

But how can it be otherwise? Doesn't Paul challenge us to "count others better than yourselves" (v. 3)?

"Wait a minute," someone says. "Surely the television evangelists are not supposed to consider their competitors better than themselves. Surely the Fundamentalists are not to consider the Charismatics better than themselves. How could the Nazarenes think the Baptists are better? And surely—oh, surely—Protestants are not being asked to think Catholics are better than themselves! There must be some other way to interpret what Paul says here."

Yes, I think there is another interpretation. But it is even more troublesome than the literal interpretation. This "sophisticated" interpretation runs as follows:

So long as we are functioning in the ordinary competitive mode of the world, it is natural for us to compare ourselves with each other. When we do, we conclude that we really are better than some other Christians—but we are going to be humble about it. In humility we will act as though they are better than us, even though we know better.

The attitude that produces this sort of interpretation is far removed from the Spirit of Christ.

A Charismatic evangelist of great influence is exposed for moral failure. His position of leadership is lost; his communications empire is threatened. *But we are not like that,* we say to ourselves. *We wouldn't do that. We wouldn't live so extravagantly or so flamboyantly. Of course not! We would be less self-serving and less lustful. We would be more careful and more responsible. And we certainly would have more personal integrity.*

In this mode of comparative thinking, we still function in worldly ways. We embrace worldly goals and worldly perceptions of reality. We adopt the procedures of the business world. We follow the ego motivations of fallen Adam. (We may edit them slightly and spiritualize them by use of the Bible; but we basically handle our religious convictions with worldly presuppositions.) We think, *They are more worldly, but we are more humble. . . . They are more liberal, but we are more conservative. . . . They are more strict, but we are more spiritual. . . .*

Yet Paul says, "There is no distinction. . . . all have sinned and fall short of the glory of God" (Rom. 3:22–23).

● **Sharing the Spirit of Christ**

Jesus turns our whole world upside down. The beautiful Christian hymn of Philippians 2:6–11 begins with the preexistence of Christ, tells of his earthly humiliation, and concludes with his exaltation in glory. We can be so struck by the beauty of it that we overlook why Paul included it here. If we take seriously what he says about Christ, however, it will revolutionize our worldly ways of thinking.

What does the hymn say about Christ? And what does it say about us?

First, it says that Christ the eternal Son was in the form of God and equal with God, but did not cling to his divine privileges; he let them go. The same truth is expressed in 2 Corinthians 8:9, where Paul is speaking about offerings in the church: "For you know the grace of our Lord Jesus Christ, that though he was rich, yet for your sake he became poor, so that by his poverty·you might become rich."

Paul does not digress into an extended discussion of Christ's preexistence or his earthly ministry. He emphasizes instead the awesome contrast between Christ's humility and our human pride. He who was in the form of God took the form of a servant. He emptied himself in voluntary poverty to become one with us in our humanity and to live among us as our servant. He did not demand the benefits of his divine office. He chose the way of humble, obedient servanthood—and he followed it all the way to death, even death on a cross.

"Therefore God has highly exalted him and bestowed on him the name which is above every name . . . " (v. 9). Jesus humbled himself—all the way. The Father exalted him—all the way. *Never did Jesus exalt himself.* Even his resurrection and ascension were not his own doing; the Father raised him from the dead and exalted him in glory. So in this profound hymn to Christ, Paul makes a direct connection between Christ's self-humiliation and the Father's exaltation.

Second, Paul talks about the impact of Christ's life on us. He says the Lord of glory humbled himself to serve and die and rise again in order to create a community of faithful people who share his Spirit. That community (namely, the church) is to be controlled by the pattern of self-effacement and humility that Jesus' incarnation and cross supremely exemplify.

I wonder whether we can grasp the incredibly radical character of Paul's simple phrase, "Have this mind among yourselves, which you have in Christ Jesus" (v. 5). The mind of Christ—i.e., Jesus' way of thinking—contradicts our ideas about the power and glory of God. Moreover, it contradicts our ideas of our own power and glory. The mind of Christ is an attitude of self-emptying; it is a mind of humility, obedience, and servanthood. It is a way of thinking that trusts God to take care of our exaltation, rather than seeking it for ourselves. I wonder whether we will ever be able to grasp the full implications of that.

Paul does not ask us to imitate Christ or follow his example. He does not say, "Jesus humbled himself; now you should humble yourself." He does not present us with a Christ we are to copy.

Instead, he lifts up a Christ whose Spirit we may share. Our growing likeness to Jesus Christ is not the product of our efforts to be humble, but the result of our obedient response to the working of his Holy Spirit in our lives. Of course Jesus is our great example, and we are to be like him. But if character emulation is what Christianity is all about, we have a religion of morality, not a gospel of grace.

Paul describes a way of thinking that is ours only as we are in Christ, only as we live in fellowship with him and his church. Paul calls for a reversal of our customary way of thinking—a revolutionary perception of reality that can be ours when Christ lives within us, transforming and renewing our minds (Rom. 12:1–2).

For example, Paul's own understanding could come only from his having Christ's perspective of his situation. Paul's idea that his imprisonment had really furthered the gospel did not result from the usual human way of thinking. His attitude that could rejoice in the preaching of Christ, even by those who were envious of other preachers, was not typical of the human spirit. His desire for Christ to be honored with his body, whether by life or death, did not come from his simply trying to follow the example of Jesus. These ideas and attitudes could come only by Paul's sharing of the Spirit of the Christ, who honors the Father in life and in death.

It would be easier to obey a set of rules telling us how to be Christlike, wouldn't it?—if we could follow such rules, check our progress, evaluate ourselves and others by them, and feel pretty good about ourselves. Instead, we are confronted with the Jesus described by Matthew, Mark, Luke, and John. We have seen how he approaches the problems of life. We know how he thinks and loves and obeys. We understand that he laid aside the splendor of living in his Father's presence to come and live among us. This Jesus cannot be imitated; he cannot be copied by any strict discipline. But his way of thinking can be ours as we share his life, his mind, and his Spirit.

How can Christians ever have one mind and one heart? We cannot—not of ourselves. It is as simple as that. The sooner we recognize this, the better. Only as we share the Spirit of Christ can the mind of Christ control us.

● Discussion Questions

1. Why do you suppose Paul makes such a strong appeal to the Philippians' feelings and affections in his call for the unity of the church?
2. Paul challenges the Philippians to have the same mind. Does this mean they should all think the same thing?
3. From your reading of the Epistle to the Philippians, what would you say were the sources of division in the church? Do you think I have exaggerated the danger of division in the church today?
4. I have said that differences of viewpoint or different ways of thinking, by themselves, do not divide us. Do you agree? To what extent can the church tolerate such differences and still be united?
5. Do you think my illustration of the church committee meeting is a valid example of a futile effort at unity? What other examples might you give?
6. Is Paul asking people of each denomination to think others are better than they (for instance, is he asking the Baptists to think the Methodists are better)? If not, what *is* he asking for?
7. I have tried to show that, though we may not have the same extravagant lifestyles that some Christian celebrities have pursued, we often act from the same motives. We may live on a more modest level, but does that make us any different if we judge ourselves by the same worldly standards of success? Discuss.

8. Paul summons us to a radical change of perspective—the Jesus way of thinking. How would you describe this? Do you agree that we are not expected to imitate Jesus? Why or why not?

9. Paul's great doctrinal statements are often tied to very practical matters. For example, Philippians 2:6–11 is related to the unity of the church; 4:13 is related to Paul's personal contentment; and 4:19 comes out of Paul's discussion of the Philippians' use of money. His profound theological statement of 1 Corinthians 8:6 is made while he talks about eating habits; 2 Corinthians 8:9 is set in a discussion about offerings. What does this suggest about the way we should teach doctrine today?

CHAPTER · 6

Fear and Trembling

Therefore, my beloved, as you have always obeyed, so now, not only in my presence but much more in my absence, work out your own salvation with fear and trembling; for God is at work in you, both to will and to work for his good pleasure.

Do all things without grumbling or questioning, that you may be blameless and innocent, children of God without blemish in the midst of a crooked and perverse generation, among whom you shine as lights in the world, holding fast the word of life, so that in the day of Christ I may be proud that I did not run in vain or labor in vain. Even if I am to be poured as a libation upon the sacrificial offering of your faith, I am glad and rejoice with you all. Likewise you also should be glad and rejoice with me (Phil. 2:12–18).

● Paul's reference to his "absence" may be a hint of his impending death. If so, these words are especially grave. But I think there's another way of looking at this passage: Perhaps Paul feared that a "hero cult" was developing around him, in which case his absence might be a blessing to the church!

Certainly, Paul's visits to Philippi were occasions of mutual affection and joy. His presence among them as an apostle could only add influence to the fledgling church. But perhaps Paul saw within himself a tendency to bind the young Christians to himself and his authority. That's an inevitable temptation for an evangelist or pastor of any influence. At the same time, many laypeople would like to have a leader whom they can follow blindly, without having to solve for themselves the bewildering problems of life.

Perhaps Paul saw this pattern developing in his relationship with the Christians at Philippi. If so, it was better for him to stay away.

Paul did have apostolic authority and he used it—much to the dismay of his opponents—to instruct and direct the life of the young churches. But if anyone is to develop a personal dependency upon the Lord, she or he must learn to depend less on the persons who taught about him. That process is difficult for both the disciple and the teacher. It's like the painful process of releasing our children to become adults.

I sense some of Paul's pain in his absence from the Philippians. If he is not to be their pastor, he wants all the more for them to be obedient to Christ and to "work out their own salvation" in fearful awareness of what God is doing among them. His phrase, "as you have always obeyed," reminds us that every Christian must be obedient to Christ. The heavenly Father's work of salvation is accomplished in the context of obedience to his Son. And it is through obedience to him that the church is to be saved.

Yet I believe we have often misunderstood the intent of Paul's statement, "Work out your own salvation with fear and trembling" (2:12). So let's consider three facets of what he is saying: (1) *the need for the church's salvation,* (2) *the importance of godly fear,* and (3) *the awareness that God is at work in the church.*

• The Church Needs to Be Saved

First, Paul says Christians must give attention not only to their personal salvation, but to the salvation of the entire body of believers. When he says, "Work out your own *salvation,*" he is using that word in the broad sense of God's good work we discussed in chapter 1. *Salvation* here refers to wholeness, health, deliverance, well-being, safety, and security, as well as to salvation from sin and a trusting relationship with God.

Remember that Paul is writing to a church wracked with dissension and division. The salvation they need is not simply the assurance of being saved in heaven, but the health and wholeness of the church body on earth. Paul says that congregational health is characterized by "being of the same mind, having the same love, being in full accord and of one mind," with nothing done "from selfishness or conceit," but with the new attitude that is ours "in Christ Jesus" (2:1–5). The church must do whatever is necessary for that harmony to prevail. That is the crux of the salvation of the Philippian church.

It is the essence of salvation for our modern church as well. We will never be the instruments of salvation that God intends us to be until we are saved—that is, until we experience health, harmony, and well-being in the church body. The mind of Christ must be at work in the body before it can be expressed to a pagan world.

What must be done if your church is to be saved? What would it take for your congregation to be whole, well, forgiven and forgiving, of one heart and mind? That's the nature of the salvation that you are called to "work out" in your congregation.

● Work With Fear and Trembling

Second, Paul says we are to work out our salvation "with fear and trembling." The Hebrew words for *fear* and *trembling* are found throughout the Old Testament, covering a range of emotions from terror to reverent awe. Most often these terms refer to a person's attitude toward God, but they are used as well to describe one's attitude toward human beings.

In the New Testament the phrase "fear and trembling" occurs five times in Paul's letters and once in the Gospel of Mark. The woman who was healed of her hemorrhage when she touched Jesus' garment came before him with "fear and trembling" (Mark 5:33). But it is significant that each time Paul uses the phrase he refers to our relations with other men and women, rather than our relations with God.

He says he came to the Corinthians, not "in lofty words or wisdom," but "in weakness and in much fear and trembling"

(1 Cor. 2:1, 3). The Corinthians later received Titus with "fear and trembling" (2 Cor. 7:15).

He exhorts the Ephesians to "be subject to one another out of reverence for Christ" (Eph. 5:21). He then applies this idea to various social relationships: wives to husbands, husbands to wives, children to parents, slaves to masters, and masters to slaves. He instructs slaves to "be obedient to those who are your earthly masters, with fear and trembling, in singleness of heart, as to Christ" (Eph. 6:5).

Paul's fifth use of the phrase is here in Philippians 2. He is writing to a divided church that needs to deal with the problems destroying its unity. He says they are to deal with one another "with fear and trembling." In view of the self-emptying example of Jesus, who came to love and serve us, the Philippians should approach one another with fear and trembling. They should deal with one another, not slavishly or self-degradingly, but in humility and mutual respect. No doubt the idea of having fear and trembling toward God is in the background of what Paul says. But this fundamental posture toward God is to define Christians' posture toward one another.

The God whom we approach in awe and reverence has come in poverty to redeem us. We should act toward one another as he acts toward us. I once read in C. S. Lewis's writings that if we could see how beautiful other Christians will be in heaven, we would bow down before them in awe and wonder. Paul says we should have some measure of that attitude toward one another now.

War, terrorism, and crime blatantly declare the low regard we have for the persons around us. So does the poisoning of our environment for the sake of profit; the manipulative way we relate to one another; our disregard of the poor, hungry, and hurting people of our world; our dependency on alcoholism and drug abuse; our tendency toward wife abuse, child abuse, and suicide— all are evidence of our failure to have reverence for other human beings and for ourselves.

I fear that we are so locked into the way things are, so accustomed to using our religion to support our prejudices, that we cannot really understand the humble way God has come to us in Jesus. We know Christ's teachings about turning the other cheek, being kind to our enemies, and giving the cup of cold water. But we really do not understand them at all.

Christ cut across our customary ways of dealing with one another. He emptied himself of his own reputation. He knelt before us and washed our feet.

The apostle Paul summons us to behave toward one another with that same attitude—"with fear and trembling." Wouldn't it be easier to have fear and trembling toward God, but deal with one another as the situation demanded? But Paul says it cannot be so.

More than we know, we have absorbed the world's devaluation of the individual. We say that one soul is more valuable than all the world's goods; we sing that Jesus would have come to die if there had been only one person to save. But we don't act as though we believe it.

This passage requires us to discern the supreme worth of each person. It speaks of those in our Christian fellowship and those outside it. It directs us to see each person with awe and respect, as though we viewed the world through the eyes of the self-emptying servant, Jesus. The church body can be healthy only as it breathes this atmosphere of awe and respect for each individual.

• God Is Working Among Us

Third, Paul says, " . . . God is at work among you, both to will and to work for his good pleasure" (v. 13). Three times in verses 12–13 (and again in verse 16) he uses various Greek words for *work*. The first word means "to achieve or accomplish something." The next two words, referring to God's work, mean "to energize" or "to operate efficiently." The last word, referring to Paul, is the word for "wearisome labor and toil." For all of his emphasis on grace, Paul is not afraid to talk about work! We might paraphrase verses 12–13 as follows:

Work to accomplish the healing of the divisions among you until there is wholeness in the body. As Christ was among us in lowliness and servanthood, be toward one another in an attitude of reverence and deep respect. Your working is not your own, for God is the energizing force, actively working to achieve his will in your fellowship.

A friend of mine served on the official board of a divided church. A new pastor had been called, but had not yet arrived. At first, the board's consensus was that the first task of the new pastor should be to bring the church together. Then they had a better thought: *It is not the new pastor's task to unite this church. That is our task. Whatever it takes to get us together, let's do it, so that when our new pastor comes we can begin to do what God wants us to do in this community.* Their inspiration may have come straight from Philippians 2:12–13. But no amount of inspiration could substitute for the plain hard work that had to be done to bring about the unity and wholeness that were that church's salvation.

The most difficult task in working out our own salvation is submitting to the lordship of Christ Jesus. The work of letting go our false pretenses and preconceived notions, the work of treating other people with fear and trembling—that is hard work indeed! Karl Barth said that in the kingdom of Christ, anyone who attempts to put his salvation into practice will be placed in a position of humility. That's never easy to accept.

What good news it is, then, to know that God is working among us! All of our working is really an obedient response to his energizing presence. When we attempt to achieve salvation in our own way, we offend one another with our assertiveness and vanity. But God can be the dynamic presence among us. He can be the person "between" us. When he is present in our relationships, he enables us to have the same mind and the same love and to live in full accord.

• Without Complaining

Because God is accomplishing everything good that happens among us, we are to "do all things without grumbling or questioning" (v. 14). Many of us would gladly do without these words! We would like to call them unrealistic and idealistic—except we remember that they were written by an innocent man in prison.

The phrase "grumbling or questioning" recalls two Old Testament episodes. After the Exodus, as the Israelites traveled toward Mount Sinai, "the whole congregation of the people of Israel murmured against Moses and Aaron in the wilderness." And Moses said, "The LORD has heard your murmurings" (Exod. 16:2, 8). After leaving Sinai, "the people complained in the hearing of the LORD about their misfortunes; and when the LORD heard it, his anger was kindled, and the fire of the LORD burned among them" (Num. 11:1). In the Israelites' murmuring there was no room for faith, no room for thankfulness, no place for fear and trembling toward God or man. God was present among them to will and to work for his good pleasure; but his presence became a burning fire because they grumbled against him.

The life of the first-century church was threatened when "the Hellenists murmured against the Hebrews because their widows were neglected in the daily distribution" (Acts 6:1). In 1 Corinthians, Paul puts grumbling on a par with idolatry, immorality, and putting the Lord to the test. He shows that each of these sins, in Old Testament times, received the judgment of God (1 Cor. 10:6–10).

When Paul says, "Stop complaining," we're apt to add this to the list of other dos and don'ts that we carry around with us. However, his words indicate something more important. I see two great realities behind this statement: the working of God in the church and the witness of the church in the world.

God is working, the world is watching, and the church is complaining!

True, we have much to complain about and to question. But our self-centered murmurs deny the energizing presence of God. They frustrate the grace of God, who is at work in all things for our good (Rom. 8:28). Our murmuring is a solemn offense to God.

We must have an inner loyalty to the Light of the World and live as his lights in the world—lights which other people see and follow.

This is why Paul tells the Philippians they are to work out their own salvation. They are to "put their house in order" by getting rid of petty strife and contention so that they can fulfill the purpose of God. By doing this, they will show themselves to be a community that lives above reproach from the world.

When Paul says the church is to be "blameless and innocent" and "without blemish," he is not depicting a perfect little commune that lives aloof from the wicked outside world. He portrays a sincere and ethically blameless community, "holding fast the word of life" (2:15–16). Christians live in the "midst of a crooked and perverse generation," among whom they are to "shine as lights in the world" (v. 15). And here Paul reminds us of what Jesus said: "You are the salt of the earth, . . . You are the light of the world" (Matt. 5:13–14).

The church must be the church in the midst of a wicked world. It must be such a different community that it illuminates the life of the world, rather than giving offense or misleading the world. Obviously, this is not always true of the church. As someone has said, remarkably good people can make their goodness remarkably unattractive by the ungraciousness of their ways.

And who would not say "amen" to this child's prayer, "O Lord, make all the bad people good and please make all the good people nice"?

Paul's prayer, however, is not merely for an increase of nice people in the world. He prays that Christian people will unhinge themselves from the self-centered and complaining of a childish world so they can be people who hold fast the Word of Life.

A Scotsman was asked what evidences had convinced him to become a Christian. He replied, "I am a Christian because the Reverend Doctor Marcus Dods is a Christian. If you wish to talk about the evidences of Christianity, Dods is one."

God desires to make us a community of such persons. For the sake of such a community, Paul would gladly pour out his life. For

71

the wholeness of such a community, we are called to work. Such communities of faith are lights in the world.

• Discussion Questions

1. What do you think Paul means when he refers to his "absence" from the Philippian church? Why does he refer to it so often (at least four times) in this short letter?
2. So often we confuse "winning people to ourselves" with winning people to Christ. How can this sort of thing be avoided?
3. Does the phrase "as you have always obeyed" (v. 12) refer to the Philippians' obedience to Paul or to God? Explain.
4. I believe *salvation* in this passage refers to the health and wholeness of the church, rather than to personal salvation. What do you think about this?
5. Do you agree that "fear and trembling" in this passage does not describe our attitude toward God but our attitude toward one another? Why or why not? What other phrases in the New Testament tell us how we are to relate to one another? (See Gal. 6:1–5; Eph. 4:32; Col. 3:12–15.)
6. How are we to "work out our own salvation" in the local church? What are we to do?
7. Why are grumbling and questioning such significant problems from Paul's point of view?
8. How do you think the world views the church? Should the world's opinion of us have any effect on what we think of ourselves or what changes we ought to make in church life?
9. I do not think the world expects the church to be perfect; but what does the world expect of us? In what ways can we be "lights in the world"?

CHAPTER · 7

Ordinary Christian Life

I hope in the Lord Jesus to send Timothy to you soon, so that I may be cheered by news of you. I have no one like him, who will be genuinely anxious for your welfare. They all look after their own interests, not those of Jesus Christ. But Timothy's worth you know, how as a son with a father he has served with me in the gospel. I hope therefore to send him just as soon as I see how it will go with me; and I trust in the Lord that shortly I myself shall come also.

I have thought it necessary to send to you Epaphroditus my brother and fellow worker and fellow soldier, and your messenger and minister to my need, for he has been longing for you all, and has been distressed because you heard that he was ill. Indeed he was ill, near to death. But God had mercy on him, and not only on him but on me also, lest I should have sorrow upon sorrow. I am the more eager to send him, therefore, that you may rejoice at seeing him again, and that I may be less anxious. So receive him in the Lord with all joy; and honor such men, for he nearly died for the work of Christ, risking his life to complete your service to me (Phil. 2:19–30).

● If these verses were not in the Bible, we would say they were quite ordinary. They speak of the goings and comings of Paul's associates between Philippi and his place of imprisonment. They express feelings of love and affirmation, of sickness and health, of uncertainty and anxiety, of joy and sorrow. Paul is not preaching or exhorting; he is writing frankly and openly about himself, Timothy, Epaphroditus, and their activities and relationships. There is no "golden text" here.

That, in fact, is why we should study these verses. They tell us in ordinary words about ordinary life under the lordship of Jesus.

If we were the Christians we ought to be, what would our lives be like? There are voices aplenty to tell us! Some tell us that we would experience miracles and healings and marvelous answers to prayer if we were filled with the Holy Spirit the way we should be. We would have our financial needs met and our dreams fulfilled if we had the faith we ought to have. Others say we would be praising God all the time and for all things.

Would we carry a nine-pound Bible with an ICHTHUS (an ancient Christian symbol) on it? Would we keep a prayer journal and go to Bible study meetings? Would we learn to talk "holy talk"?

One day a young student and I were walking down to the campus chapel when he said, "Brother Welch, last night I was just *travailing* before the Lord in prayer!" I'm not sure he even knew what the word meant. But he was a committed Christian, so he wanted to use the right language.

What would *your* life be if you were all that God expected you to be? Would you watch more religious TV programs, listen to Christian tapes and records, and go to seminars? Would you witness to your neighbors how God "just opened the door" for you to buy your house at a bargain or was so good to you that he gave you a promotion and a new car? Many voices say this is how Christians should live.

But there is another voice, that of Paul. I think we would agree that he was probably the sort of Christian he ought to be. Here are some of the phrases from his letter: "that I may be cheered by news of you," "anxious for your welfare," "as soon as I see how it will go with me," "distressed because you heard that he was ill," "lest I should have sorrow upon sorrow," "that I may be less anxious." These words were written by the person who said in the same letter, "Have no anxiety about anything, but in everything by prayer and supplication with thanksgiving let your requests be made known to God" (4:6).

Paul's words tell us that the Christian life is, after all, quite ordinary. For the most part, it is made up of ordinary events—

concern for friends, uncertainties about the future, and anxieties about situations we cannot control or alleviate. If we were indeed the Christians we ought to be, our lives would probably be very much the way they are now. Yet in our desire to be what God wants us to be, in our hunger to be more "spiritual," we tend to deny the reality of our God-given life.

• Accept the Realities of Life

Two great Christian doctrines are dominant in my personal theology these days. One is creation. I believe that God is the Creator of this world, that he is my personal Creator and sustainer, and that the world he created is good and the way he arranged it is good. In the Genesis account, God said, "Let there be . . . "—and there was. When it was all done, God said, "That's very good." I believe we need to affirm that as well.

This is no denial of the fact that evil has invaded our world. Genesis tells that story, too. But we Christians believe that it is still a *good* fallen world, not an evil world. Between those two ideas is a world of difference.

God is our Creator and he made life good. It is good to be human; it is good to laugh and love and work and play. It is good to smell the flowers and see the sunset and feel the life of this good earth. It is right to fix up the house and mow the lawn and wash the dishes and go to work and pay the bills and do what ordinary life demands in our good old world, made by our good old God! If in our desire to be more Christlike we turn away from the world as it is, we put God against God. If in pursuit of God, we flee from the present realities of God's creation, where are we to find the ordinary gifts of life he has given us?

I think most of us would say that God's most precious gift is children. Yet I think all of us would say that the hardest thing on our religious life is raising those children. Strange, isn't it? Nothing can create more guilt or a greater sense of spiritual failure than trying to raise a family of small children. God's precious gifts can become barriers between us and God. Does this mean we have misunderstood children? or have we simply misunderstood the Christian life? We know that the Christian life demands discipline, devotion, and self-denial. But we must not deny the way God has made this world in our search for real relationship with him.

The other great doctrine that undergirds my understanding of the Christian life is incarnation—the doctrine that the eternal sovereign Creator, God the Father, has himself entered into our world's history in the person of Jesus. This Jesus, who is one with the Father in his divinity, has become one with us in our humanity. He came into our real world and into our humanity to save us. He walked with real feet on real dirt and lived a genuine human life.

He spent his growing, maturing years in a carpenter shop. Do we believe that sometime along the way he hit his thumb with a mallet—and said, "Shalom!" Of course! Those years of hard labor sanctified our own work for daily bread. The lovely old words of the Methodist marriage ritual remind us that Jesus' presence at the wedding in Cana in Galilee "adorned and beautified" the "holy estate" of matrimony for us. In the Upper Room, the Savior used ordinary Passover bread and common wine in the cup to institute the sacramental meal of the new covenant.

God's incarnation means that we are saved by his entering into our common life. If we believe that the Son of God came into the world to redeem the world, we don't have to leave the world to follow him. The life we live with him and in him is quite ordinary.

● Free to Live the Ordinary Life

Paul's words also tell us that the Christian life is most extraordinary. I observe this in his use of the phrase "in the Lord Jesus" or "in the Lord." Three times he drops this comment into an otherwise ordinary statement about the evangelists' coming and going: "I hope in the Lord Jesus to send Timothy to you soon" (2:19); "I trust in the Lord that shortly I myself shall come also" (2:24); "So receive him in the Lord" (2:29).

Paul wants Timothy to bring back word from Philippi so that he will be cheered up—and he is hoping in the Lord Jesus. He doesn't know how things will turn out in prison, but he wants to visit the Philippians again—and he is trusting in the Lord. He wants Epaphroditus to return to them so they will be happy and he will be less anxious—"so receive him in the Lord."

Jesus is Lord of our ordinary life, and that is most extraordinary. The lordship of Jesus coexists with our coming and going, uncertainty, illness, anxiety, and hope. Evidently, his lordship is not exercised in some ideal spiritual realm above our common early experience. Jesus reigns in the normal flow of ordinary life. That does not make our life extraordinary. But the fact that Jesus comes to be with us in our ordinary life—that is extraordinary. We are free to follow him through the common life he sanctified, through the routine life that he blessed.

The presence of the Lord Jesus in Paul's prison cell does not seem to stifle his free and natural expressions of hope, uncertainty, and anxiety. Jesus' lordship does not eliminate unexpected illness or the threat of death. Paul has the freedom, under the lordship of Jesus, to say what he feels and be what he is. He does not need to cover his emotions. He does not need to speak in proverbs or platitudes. Jesus is Lord.

Let's consider some implications of this. Since Jesus is Lord of the ordinary life, we don't need to hype our Christian testimony. That is, we do not need to exaggerate our feelings or experiences as we speak about them, in order to prove our faith. Our lives, under Christ's lordship, need not be sensational or spectacular. We are free to be real in the real world the way it is. We are free to go to church and worship God "in spirit and in truth." We may bring our real selves into his presence to praise and thank him without having to be entertained extravagantly. The presence of God is God's, the glory of God is God's glory, not open to manipulation, not subject to our control. And not always amenable to our expectations.

This is a serious issue. Our belief in creation and incarnation affirms that the whole of life is sacramental. That is, the real experiences of normal human life are means of God's grace. We do not need to create a "spiritual atmosphere" by artificial means to know that God is present. The glory of God is not only present in his sanctuary, but everywhere. Jesus is Lord.

And so it is in daily life. If you dedicate your kitchen to God, do not expect the glow of heaven to rest upon it when you cook and clean up. If you offer your workbench or office to God, do not think that heavenly peace will always surround it. Jesus is already Lord of both your home and your work. He is sanctifying those experiences as they are.

We tend to assume that if we belong to Christ and seek to bring our whole lives under his sovereignty, life will not be ordinary anymore; we will be lifted above the common level of existence through the transforming radiance of God's Spirit. But we should give up such assumptions. Headaches still hurt in our heads. And when our feelings get hurt, we still feel it in the pit of the stomach.

I talked with a friend who was suffering a terminal illness. He was not an optimistic person and certainly not in an optimistic mood. He said, "The worst thing about this is not that I know I am going to die. Everyone has to die. The hardest thing for me is that I don't think I'm facing it the way a Christian should. I'm not as triumphant as I ought to be."

He had to bear the pain of his illness, the burden of his coming death—and the guilt of not being triumphant. What a tragic reversal of grace!

He believed that being a Christian meant being triumphant. He was not being triumphant; so was he still a Christian? And he was sick unto death. What an awful burden to bear at such a time! I hope our long talks were helpful to him. They were profoundly insightful to me. I understood in a new way what an intolerable burden being a "victorious Christian" can be.

A few weeks later, outside my friend's hospital room, a minister said to me, "Something is wrong. There ought to be more of the presence of God here. What a marvelous opportunity to show the world how a Christian dies!"

There it was again—the false assumption that if Jesus is present, pain is somehow transformed into virtue, and suffering is made radiant. But my friend was not on the Mount of Transfiguration. He was in Gethsemane, crying to his Father out of the depths of despair, in the agony of death—no radiant glow, no sound of angels' wings. Just the light in the ceiling and the sounds of pumps and monitors and the squeaking of nurses' shoes on waxed floors. Just the subdued voices of loved ones, saying quiet nothings. And the presence of the Lord Jesus—in that very room.

I have come to believe that our cryings and complainings to God are as much expressions of faith in him as are our songs of praise. I tried to help my friend let his weight down on the everlasting arms. I tried to help him cry his cries and fear his fears and complain his complaints and ask his whys. I wanted to help him trust his heavenly Father enough to moan and groan and whine, as well as praise and pray and sing.

Are we really trusting God if we can only praise him? Can we be confident enough in his love to feel our genuine feelings and be in his presence the way we are? The results of faith are not always seen in miracles, opened doors, answered prayers, and peace of mind. They are also evident in the patient endurance of pain, in loss, in disappointment, and in uncertainty. They are seen in the offering of our everyday life to him. Faith is seen in our confidence to express our real selves and our real feelings to him.

We need to go back to the Book of Psalms and read again the laments that speak so deeply to our souls. Not Psalm 23. I mean the ones that cry out to God from distress, sickness, and hardship. I mean the ones that say, "O God, where are you when I need you? Why is my soul in the darkness of distress? I am alone, and no one cares. Why do things go well with the wicked rich, and I languish in pain and sorrow? My so-called friends have forsaken me. I am desperate and alone. No one cares." Those are the psalms we need to read again if we want to understand the nature of real trust in God.

The lament psalms are not complaints *about* God; they are complaints *to* God. The psalmist's relationship with him is such that he can say what he feels with total honesty. After pouring out his bitter complaint, he closes these psalms with great affirmations of trust and confidence: "O Lord, you are my rock. You are my strength. My hope is in you. You are ever with me, my shield and defender. Your love is faithful. I will praise you."

Can we praise God if we cannot complain to him? Can we laugh if we cannot cry? Can we really love if we cannot be angry? The lordship of Jesus in our common life means that we are not weighted with the intolerable burden of being uncommon. We are not faced with the impossible task of being radiant. We are what we are, we experience what we experience—good, bad, or indifferent—and Jesus is Lord.

● Free to Care in Ordinary Ways

Paul reveals another way in which the Christian life is extraordinary. Jesus is present in our caring for one another. Most people look out for their own interests; they do not care about the things of Jesus Christ. But Paul says Timothy is different. He cares about the Philippians (2:19–22). Timothy cares about them and is anxious for them, and Paul equates that anxious care with a concern for the things of Jesus Christ.

How does anyone "look after" the interests of Jesus Christ? What are the Lord's interests? In this case, Christ's interest is the wholeness of the Philippian church. So Timothy is eager to "look after" those interests.

How many of us assume that Christ is interested only in prayer, worship, praise, and an awareness of the Holy Spirit's presence and power? How many of us feel some sense of distance from Christ and his church because we are not at home in an atmosphere of emotional prayer and praise? This passage of Scripture has a word to both sides of the question: Christ cares about his people. And so he is present in our concern for one another. That is most extraordinary.

Paul makes the same point when he writes of Epaphroditus. Here is his story: Paul was in prison. The Philippians learned about it and decided to gather up a package of supplies to send to their friend. They sent it by Epaphroditus, who got desperately ill and was unable to return to them. They thought he would die— but he didn't, thank God. He was finally able to go home again. He took with him the letter we know as Paul's Epistle to the Philippians.

Paul says of these simple events: "He nearly died for the work of Christ" (2:30); "I am filled, having received from Epaphroditus the gifts you sent, a fragrant offering, a sacrifice acceptable and pleasing to God" (4:18). The man delivering the goods got sick. It was as simple as that. No, it wasn't as simple as that. He risked his life for Christ, so his errand to Paul was a fragrant, sacrificial offering that was pleasing to God.

Let us bring this example up to date. Mrs. Johnson's husband left her with a house full of children, bills, and empty cupboards. Mrs. Pressley got concerned and rallied the church folks to donate food, clothes, and money. So she gathered it up, stacked it in her car, and drove over to Mrs. Johnson's.

On the way she had a terrible wreck; the car was totaled, and she ended up in the hospital. It looked as if she would die—but she didn't, thank God. She got better and went back to help her neighbor in other ways.

As we relate such a story, we naturally speak in terms of goodwill and kindness, the concern of a friend, the love of a church, the tragedy of an accident, and the community's gratitude for Mrs. Pressley's recovery. Paul would speak in terms of looking after the interests of Jesus Christ—of risking one's life for Christ, of fragrant offerings and sacrifices to God. In doing so, he would remind us that ordinary Christian life is most extraordinary because what we do for one another, we do for Christ. The Lord told us the same thing: "And the King will answer them, 'Truly, I say to you, as you did it to one of the least of these my brethren, you did it to me'" (Matt. 25:40).

Some individuals send cards to people who are sick and hurting. Others say, "What can I do to help?" Some visit inmates in prison or take clothes and food to needy people. Some sweep the floors in the fellowship hall, set up for the potlucks, and clean up afterward. Others bathe, feed, and keep on being kind to those who are infirm and aged. I hope they know Jesus is with them. I hope they realize that he is where they are, the Lord of ordinary life, glorified in the common caring for others.

Well, what of your ordinary life? The apostle calls you to open it up to the lordship of Jesus, just the way it is.

We know that the Lord of glory was incarnate in human flesh and walked among us in human ways and accomplished his Father's purpose through the self-emptying and agony of the cross. He calls us to follow him through the common life he sanctified, the ordinary life he blessed. He calls us to love and care for one another in everyday ways because we know he is present, and our service is unto him. That is most extraordinary. It makes room for us to experience his radiance and his triumph in unexpected ways.

• Discussion Questions

1. If you were the Christian God wanted you to be, what kind of life would you lead? Does this question cause you to think in terms of miracles, triumphs, or answers to prayer? Explain.
2. I stated that if you were all that God wanted you to be, your life would be much the way it is now. How do you react to that statement? Of course, that statement is not universally true, because the Lord is calling some Christians to radical change. But in what respect is the statement true of every Christian?
3. How do you reconcile Paul's words about anxiety in 2:28 with those in 4:6?
4. I said that we need to realize the difference between an evil world and a good world that is fallen. Do you agree? Why would such a distinction be important?
5. How do the doctrines of creation and incarnation affect the nature of the Christian life?
6. What are some ways we set "God against God" in our efforts to live the Christian life?
7. A key idea of this chapter is that Jesus is Lord of the ordinary life, but that does not mean the ordinary life becomes extraordinary.

Why do we tend to think something must be wrong if our lives in Christ are plain and ordinary?

8. What would you have told my friend who was terminally ill? Should he have been more triumphant? How would you have responded to the minister outside the hospital room?

9. Do you agree that we are free to express to God both our praise and our anger, our faith and our doubt?

10. Some lament psalms are 22, 25, 31, 83, 42, and 43. What other psalms are favorites of yours? Why are they meaningful to you?

CHAPTER · 8
Loss and Gain

Finally, my brethren, rejoice in the Lord. To write the same things to you is not irksome to me, and is safe for you.

Look out for the dogs, look out for the evil-workers, look out for those who mutilate the flesh. For we are the true circumcision, who worship God in spirit, and glory in Christ Jesus, and put no confidence in the flesh. Though I myself have reason for confidence in the flesh also. If any other man thinks he has reason for confidence in the flesh, I have more: circumcised on the eighth day, of the people of Israel, of the tribe of Benjamin, a Hebrew born of Hebrews; as to the law a Pharisee, as to zeal a persecutor of the church, as to righteousness under the law blameless. But whatever gain I had, I counted as loss for the sake of Christ. Indeed I count everything as loss because of the surpassing worth of knowing Christ Jesus my Lord. For his sake I have suffered the loss of all things, and count them as refuse, in order that I may gain Christ and be found in him, not having a righteousness of my own, based on law, but that which is through faith in Christ, the righteousness from God that depends on faith (Phil. 3:1–9).

● Philippians 3 begins with a call to rejoice in the Lord. Nine times already Paul has spoken of joy and rejoicing. The words express Paul's joyful relationship with the Philippians and his concern that the problems of the church not erode the quality of their joyful relationship with Christ.

But another threat to their joy is indicated by the sudden change of mood and the sharp terms Paul uses in 3:2, "Look out for the dogs . . . the evil workers . . . those who mutilate the flesh." He is sounding an alarm against Jewish Christians (called Judaizers) who taught that, in addition to believing in Christ, a Christian must keep the law and observe the Jewish religious rights such as circumcision.

For the Jews, the word *dogs* was a synonym for *unclean*. Gentiles were called "dogs" by pious orthodox Jews. The Judaizers were seeking for cleanness by their efforts at keeping law and ceremony; but Paul perceived that these very efforts rendered their quest for cleanness unclean. Those who worked so hard to be religiously superior were actually working evil, because of their ego-motivated labors. Their pride in circumcision (meant to be a sign of their covenant relationship with God) rendered it a physical mutilation, having no spiritual significance at all. Everything was turned upside down because they were operating from self, for self. They were people "of the flesh."

Do we realize that the judgment of God is upon all our self-efforts to be right with him?

Our efforts to gain merit block the flow of God's grace into our lives and bring us under his condemnation. The problem is not our effort to please God; it is the fact that our goodness is spawned by ego, crowned with pride, and utilized to gain divine approval. The self-serving quest for cleanness produces uncleanness. The labor for righteousness produces evil. Sacred religious rights and ceremonies distort the very relationship they seek to engender. All of these problems result from our ego-motivated religious activities.

• The Marks of Authentic Christianity

Paul goes on to describe authentic Christianity. First, it involves the worship or service of God in Spirit. Whatever outward forms or ceremonies may be used, the indispensable qualification for true worship is that it be done "in spirit and truth" (John 4:23).

Only the Spirit of God can inspire true worship of God. When we worship, the Spirit reminds us of our complete dependence upon him. This is doubtless one of the great blessings of regular Lord's Day worship. We are brought into God's presence, called to turn from ourselves and depend on our "Maker, Redeemer, and Friend."

Second, authentic Christianity glories in Christ Jesus. The real issue between Paul and his Judaizing opponents at Philippi was who gets the glory. And the very same problem was destroying the church at Galatia. The sacred rite of circumcision was being used as a means of controlling the church. "They desire to have you circumcised that they may glory in your flesh. But far be it from me to glory except in the cross of our Lord Jesus Christ" (Gal. 6:13–14).

Judaizers, for the keeping of religious laws and ceremonies, gave a sense of personal well-being in relationship with God and a sense of pride in relationship with others. It is easy enough to criticize them. Their sinful self-dependence is clearly laid out for all to see. But did they see it in themselves any more than we see it in ourselves?

What gives us our sense of worth and well-being before God and others? Do we take self-satisfaction in the performance of our religious duties? These questions point to an old, old problem: We take pride in the wrong things.

> Thus says the LORD: "Let not the wise man glory in his wisdom, let not the mighty man glory in his might, let not the rich man glory in his riches; but let him who glories glory in this, that he understands and knows me, that I am the LORD who practice steadfast love, justice, and righteousness in the earth; for in these things I delight, says the LORD" (Jer. 9:23–24).

Our boasting in ourselves, even in our spiritual selves, is the essence of sin. Our glory is to be found in Jesus Christ.

Third, Paul says authentic Christians "put no confidence in the flesh" (3:3). In this context, Paul could mean that he put no trust in the physical rite of circumcision. However, he usually used the term *flesh* to refer to the whole being of a person, as one exists apart from the Spirit of God. Our *flesh* denotes our self-dependent human self, acting apart from the grace of God in what we are and do and achieve.

Paul could have boasted about his heritage. He was circumcised on the eighth day as prescribed by Jewish law (Lev. 12:3). He had a long and noble family line. "A Hebrew born of the Hebrews" was one who kept the traditional Jewish language and customs. For all Paul's connections with the Greco-Roman world of his day, he was a thoroughly "certified" Jew in the long line of certified Judaism. It is doubtful that any of the Judaizers who were pressuring the Philippian church had a more authentic heritage than he.

He could have boasted about his achievements. With regard to law keeping, he was a Pharisee, an expert and strict observer of the Jewish law. With regard to zeal, he had been a persecutor of the church; not content to keep the law himself, he tried to put down any threat to the law-tradition system. With regard to righteousness under the law, he was blameless. No one could point a finger at Paul's law-abiding life and condemn him. He had everything the Judaizers would like to take pride in. He possessed all the qualifications that for them were the source of personal satisfaction and influence. So Paul was able to meet them on their own ground and hold up his superior credentials.

Then he changed his whole approach by saying, "But whatever gain I had, I counted as loss for the sake of Christ. Indeed, I count everything as loss because of the surpassing worth of knowing Christ Jesus my Lord. For his sake I have suffered the loss of all things, and count them as refuse, in order that I may gain Christ" (3:7–8). He did not say the former values of his life were inferior. He said he counted them as loss. His whole perspective had shifted. He saw the contrast between his own inadequate righteousness and Christ's adequate righteousness; it was the difference between gain and loss, loss and gain.

As one commentator has observed, Paul discovered that in his accounts he had placed on the asset side what was actually a loss, and in his delusion he was hastening to ruin. His religious heritage and upbringing; his religious zeal and accomplishments—these seemed to be his gains. But Christ revealed his inverted values. What he had thought to be gain, he now understood to be loss.

● Righteousness Lost—and Gained

What did Paul lose, and what did he gain? He lost righteousness, and he gained righteousness. From that point of view, what he called a loss was not really lost at all.

He was still an Israelite of the tribe of Benjamin. He still had been circumcised on the eighth day. He still had the same parentage and heritage. He never said he had been a hypocrite; he had been a good person before, and he was a good person still. Yet those were the very things Paul considered to be loss. What he lost was the righteousness of his own, "based on law." What he gained was "the righteousness from God that depends on faith" (v. 9).

What do we need to be right with God, right with ourselves, and right in the human world? Paul thought he had everything right. He had the right grandparents, right nation, and right religion— and he had done right by them all. But none of this had put him to rights with God or himself. He realized that all the supposed right things were done for the benefit of himself. This fact blocked him from a real relationship with God as effectively as the sins of the ordinary Gentiles he despised.

This seems to imply that goodness is a problem, righteousness is a hindrance, and trying hard is a mistake. Not true. And yet goodness, when it is our own goodness done for merit, is a problem. Righteousness, when it is used to claim a proper standing before God, is a hindrance. And trying hard, when we're trying to "make it" by ourselves, is a mistake.

These are hard words. They fly in the face of our ordinary way of looking at religion and religious people. To accept Paul's words demands that we let go of our religious securities and our prideful self-dependence. It means that we must let go of the righteousness that comes from our own efforts, so that we can accept the righteousness we can neither earn nor deserve. Paul's message demands a radically different point of view, a drastic turnabout in our normal way of thinking. The right word for it is *repentance*— total change of our mind and perspective.

This is precisely what had happened to Paul. He came to see all his personal goodness as "refuse" or rubbish. He saw his righteousness as sin. He came to this conclusion when Christ threw his smug and tidy world into disarray. A revelation of Jesus the Christ—in Paul's case, on the road to Damascus—threw him off his feet, upset his balance, blinded him to his old perspective, and opened him up to the gift of God's grace.

Will we accept such a revelation? Can we ever let go of our ordinary ways of thinking about good heritage, good life, good intentions, and good religion? Can we see them as terribly efficient deterrents to a vital relationship with God in Christ by faith? Can we ever understand all these good things as loss—not simply a zero, but a minus? One thing is sure. Such a change will not occur without the revelation of Christ Jesus in our hearts.

We cannot come to this conclusion by changing our membership from the synagogue to the church because it offers a more liberated lifestyle. We cannot see it by deciding that circumcision or other religious rites are not that important after all. We come to the point Paul reached through a radical shift in our life perspective, created by the revelation of Christ Jesus.

• Security in Religion?

The sudden change of intensity in chapter 3 indicates the seriousness of Paul's concern for the life of the Philippian church, in lieu of the destructive influence of the Judaizers. The questions the Judaizers raised have not gone away:

- What's wrong with hanging on to Judaism and believing in Christ?
- How much law do we have to fulfill when we have been saved by grace?

• Is the purpose of God's grace to help us fulfill the law?

The growing number of Mormons, Jehovah's Witnesses, and Seventh-day Adventists testifies to the fact that the relationship of Old Testament law to faith in Christ is not a settled matter.

A fundamental issue that set Paul at odds with the Judaizers was the question of where we should find our security in religion. The Judaizers placed their keeping of the law alongside their faith in God. The ritual "extras" gave them a sense of security in the presence of God, being a sort of spiritual handle on the power of God to work on their behalf. Their religion gave them something other religious folk did not have.

We human beings have a profound need to feel secure in our relationship with God, so we find it difficult to trust in Christ alone. Converted pagans may keep a few little gods in their homes, just to be on the safe side. They think it may be well to stay on good terms with the witch doctor, just in case someone gets sick or has bad luck. One may wear a cross or carry a rabbit's foot because it is a good feeling to have the "bases covered."

Such naive examples must not blind us to our own need to place something alongside faith in Christ to give us a sense of security. Sacraments, church rituals, a life of morality, good works, or a certain lifestyle are very reassuring. Many prayers for the intervention of God are prefaced with these phrases: "O God, you know I have always gone to church and tried to do the right thing." "Lord, you know how we have worked for you and tried to do your will." "We have been faithful in giving and serving down through the years. Now, Lord, honor the faithfulness of your people by. . . . " These may be legitimate expressions of the feelings we bring to God in prayer. But the dangers of trusting our religion are very real, and they are destructive.

Through the centuries, theologians have reminded us that pride easily seeps into religion. Simcox records the story of a Carthusian monk who was talking to a stranger about his order. "We are not in a class with the Jesuits in learning. The Franciscans excel us in good works. The Dominicans are better at preaching. But when it comes to humility, we are the best!"

Everywhere Paul preached justification by grace through faith apart from works, there were some people who said, "Well, that means we can obtain forgiveness no matter how much we sin; God loves to forgive." And those on the other side of the aisle, like the Judaizers, said, "Yes, but we must also observe this or that discipline to prove or demonstrate our faith." So it is today. Our need for religious security almost compels us to support or buttress our faith in Christ by some religious ritual or lifestyle.

We feel such a need to control our lives that we tend to put ourselves at the center and bring Christ alongside for support. We find our meaning and value, our security and our fulfillment in a variety of things; then we go to church and ask for God's help with our projects. The result is the same. In the first case, we find our security in something other than Christ, such as rituals and self-imposed religious disciplines. In the second case, we place Christ alongside us for support. We find a secondary security in him; he becomes our "fallback" position.

The Judaizing Christians did both. In some instances, they put the ritual law alongside Christ; in others, they put Christ alongside the law. Sometimes they felt that authentic religion was a matter of "Christ plus law." At other times, they thought it was "law plus Christ." But in neither instance did they allow Christ to be at the center—the sole source of life's meaning and security.

There is no question as to Paul's position on this point. At the center of the Christian faith is Christ—Christ and no other security, no other affirmation, no other support, no other plea, no other rock. For Christ, the Christian gives up all else as loss. Outside of Christ, all else is trash. Paul would not betray Christ for things that really did not matter. The things that once gave meaning to his life were the very things he considered loss when loyalty to Christ was at stake.

I wonder, how many of us are putting Christ at the center of our lives—but alongside him are other dependencies? And how many of us are putting Christ alongside the real center of our life? In either case, the result is a sort of ho-hum dutiful Christianity, not real faith in him.

Isn't there a better way? Yes, there is. It is the way of total loss for total gain. It is the way of surrendering our self-righteousness in order to gain Christ's righteousness. It is the way of losing our self-dependency to gain Christ-dependency. It is the way of losing religious security to gain the assurance of living in Christ.

The glory of such a life is this: In losing what is supposed to be our gain, we in fact gain what we would have lost through our inverted values and false dependencies.

What did the Judaizers really want? What did Paul really want? For that matter, what does any religious person really want? I believe the answer is *righteousness*—a right relationship with God.

Every Christian would affirm that Christ is involved in our right relationship with God. The question is, How is he involved?

Paul harshly rejected the Judaizers, not because they rejected Christ, but because they tried to add him to their own efforts toward righteousness. He opposed them because their faith was not totally in Christ; it was in Christ *and* their obedience to the religious system.

But for Paul, the saving knowledge of Christ was the supreme reality and joy of life. It rearranged and reordered the whole of his existence. The total abandonment of his life to Christ gained for him a right relationship with God and brought him the joy of the Lord. For the sake of that relationship, he gladly surrendered all the things that were "gain" in his life. By losing them, he found the supreme gain of Christ Jesus his Lord.

I wonder, What would Paul say to us about the place Christ holds in our lives? I believe the Holy Spirit would use his words to make us consider what things are "gain" to us. The words of missionary martyr Jim Elliott come to mind: "A man is no fool who gives what he cannot keep to gain what he cannot lose."

● Discussion Questions

1. Philippians has been called "the epistle of joy." Why do you think Paul uses the words *joy* and *rejoice* so often in this letter?
2. What do you think are the "same things" he mentions in 3:1?
3. Consult Bible commentaries and Bible dictionaries to find the various interpretations of "dogs," "evil-workers," and "those who mutilate the flesh." See what they say about "Judaizers."
4. Discuss the statement "the judgment of God is upon all our self-efforts to be right with him."
5. Paul contrasts authentic Christianity with the "Christianity" of the Judaizers. Describe in your own words the three characteristics he mentions.
6. Why do you suppose Paul boasts of his heritage and achievements in this epistle? In what other epistle does he emphasize his credentials?
7. What did Paul actually lose in the "loss of all things"?
8. When we invite others to become Christians, we often say that "Christians are happier" or "Christians have real peace of mind." After reading Paul's letter, do you think these are the most important reasons for becoming a Christian?
9. Give an example of how we tend to put Christ alongside other things that give us our real sense of security.
10. What do you see as the central truth of this section of Philippians?

CHAPTER · 9

Knowing Jesus

But whatever gain I had, I counted as loss for the sake of Christ. Indeed I count everything as loss because of the surpassing worth of knowing Christ Jesus my Lord. For his sake I have suffered the loss of all things, and count them as refuse, in order that I may gain Christ and be found in him, not having a righteousness of my own, based on law, but that which is through faith in Christ, the righteousness from God that depends on faith; that I may know him and the power of his resurrection, and may share his sufferings, becoming like him in his death, that if possible I may attain the resurrection from the dead (Phil. 3:7–11).

● Paul used many terms to express the divine-human relationship made possible through Christ. *Salvation, justification, reconciliation, regeneration,* and *adoption* are a few of them. But here he uses the simple phrase, "that I may know him."

Knowing Jesus seems like a simple thing. But *know* is an open-ended word. In Scripture it can have great depth and richness of meaning, beyond our common use of the term.

Paul must have this more comprehensive meaning in mind when he makes it clear that knowing Jesus is the supreme reality of his whole existence. He says the "surpassing worth of knowing Christ Jesus" has so transformed his perspective that he can "count everything as loss . . . count them as refuse" in order to "gain Christ" (3:7–8).

What happens when we really know Jesus? I once read that real Christian experience comes about when our souls meet with

Christ—not in a brief encounter, but in a lasting relationship that is personal and unique. I've found that to be true. Knowing Jesus means having a personal relationship with him.

Because God is a person, we understand ourselves as persons. He is the ground of our own personhood. We are created in his image, and thus reflect his personhood. We are able to enter into dialogue with him. We may speak to God because he listens; and we may listen because he speaks to us, addresses us by name, and calls for our response. He has spoken to us supremely in the person of Jesus Christ, who comes to meet us and bring us into personal relationship with himself.

● Personal Fellowship With God

One of Paul's key phrases, "knowing Christ Jesus my Lord" (v. 8), describes this relationship. The personal God has taken the initiative and has come to us in the person of Jesus. We are his creatures, and he "knows" us; we are his redeemed people, and he loves us. He has made a costly commitment to us. He has approached us in humility and openness, inviting us to respond to his love and enter into personal fellowship with him. It is by responding to his offer of love in Jesus that we come to "know" God.

From this perspective, knowing God is not very different from knowing other persons.

Getting to know someone takes time; and it takes honest communication. Very soon in a new relationship, we must decide whether to continue this sharing, knowing process. That decision can lead to increasing honesty and openness, which (if we feel trusted and feel the other person is trustworthy) leads to deeper levels of commitment and self-disclosure.

The process really isn't complicated; it isn't magical, mechanical, or impossible. Two persons meet, spend some time sharing with one another, and decide to trust each other. They decide to become vulnerable to one another, to share more deeply—and so come to know each other. That is how a lasting personal relationship begins.

That is the way we may come to know Jesus Christ, and thus to know God. Of course, there are some differences:

- Jesus has already known us and loved us before we know him.
- Jesus has already deeply and truthfully opened his heart to us, in utter commitment and vulnerability.
- Jesus has pledged himself to us in the ultimate promise of the cross.
- We do not need to wonder whether Jesus' love is real or if his character is trustworthy, for he is God.

Yet Jesus begins his relationship with us in remarkably simple ways. He said to some inquiring disciples, "Come and see" (John 1:39). To others he said, "Follow me" (Mark 1:17). To one man he said, "I must stay at your house today" (Luke 19:5). To the question of another, Jesus answered, "We will come to him and make our home with him" (John 14:23).

We come to know Jesus the same way we come to know other persons: by investing some time, by engaging in some real sharing, by making an inner decision to trust, and by offering some honesty and openness. It is nothing magic, nothing mechanical, nothing impossible. It is two persons getting to know each other. Knowing him does not require that we have a certain type of religious personality. And it does not demand a stereotypical religious "experience."

Ask two friends, "How did you meet?" Their answers will vary from the ordinary to the bizarre. But ask them, "How did you get to *know* each other?" Their answers will include all the same old words: *time, sharing, openness, honesty, trust,* and *commitment.* What a magnificent monotony there is in the simple way persons get to know one another!

Monotonous may not seem to be a very good word to describe the way we come to know Jesus Christ. But perhaps it is, if it reminds us that knowing Jesus is common to our way of knowing and loving other persons. Maybe it is monotonous, in the sense that this is not a relationship reserved for special people who are capable of unusual emotions and experiences; it is a relationship that is open to us all.

• A Unique Relationship

Another dimension of our relationship with Christ is its uniqueness. A large part of Paul's own joyful assurance and a large measure of his authority in the early churches had to do with his confidence in his unique relationship with Christ. He did not get this relationship from someone else; it was not patterned after anyone else's.

We see great commonality in our worship experiences. Christening, dedication, confirmation, baptism, Lord's Supper, marriage, and funeral—these are very much the same in any setting. But each of us responds to these ceremonies in a unique way.

My relationship with Christ is mine; yours is yours. Mine is not yet what I want it to be, but such as it is, it is mine—and therefore authentic. Yours is not yet what you want it to be, nor yet what it will become by the grace of God, but such as it is, it is yours. Simply because it is not like someone else's experience does not mean it is not real.

Scripture says, "All we like sheep have gone astray" (Isa. 53:6). I am concerned that all we like sheep have followed whatever the popular evangelists and conference leaders have told us about the Christian life. We have conformed to certain patterns of belief and behavior by which we judge ourselves (and other Christians) to be in or out of the fold. Paul's simple phrase, "knowing Jesus," brings us back to the basics of Christian life. It confronts us with the reality of a *personal* relationship with Jesus Christ, made unique by virtue of the unique characteristics of each Christian.

Compared to Paul's statement, so many of our claims seem hollow. One says, "I have been baptized." Do you know Jesus? "I'm a born-again Christian." Do you know Jesus? "I've been a church member for years." Do you know Jesus? Paul regarded all the usual claims of religious folk as nothing more than "refuse," compared to knowing Jesus.

● What Difference Does It Make?

Paul's relationship with Christ had a pervasive effect upon his life. It is true, isn't it, that we are affected by the persons we know. These very words conjure up faces of loved persons who have deeply influenced us for good. Unfortunately, they also evoke memories of those who have been destructive to us. But for good or ill, we are never unaffected by the people we know. Years ago I began teaching at a Christian college with the express purpose of being to others what a revered college teacher had been to me. The way I teach and how I feel about teaching directly reflects the influence of a seminary professor who "being dead yet speaketh." And there is Jesus: think of the countless ways he has influenced the lives of countless persons, including ourselves.

In Philippians 3:10 Paul reveals four ways in which knowing Jesus made a difference in his life.

First, it meant knowing Someone who rose from the dead. The bittersweet element in any loving human relationship is the awareness of its transient character. The more profound our love, the more poignant this awareness. People move and change, and finally they die. How we wish this were not so! Over all our hopes and dreams and longings is the sign of death. The gravestone is the ultimate symbol of our transient human condition. But we know Someone who was raised from the dead! By the power of God, Jesus conquered death. He is alive and present with us, and we are inspired by his presence. He makes a living difference in our lives.

Paul often uses the word *power* in connection with Jesus' resurrection. He says that we know Jesus in the power of his resurrection; we recognize and trust the power that raised him from the dead; we see that power operative in our own lives.

This changes our perspective; it opens wide our horizons.

Nothing is ever quite the same after we know we are resurrection people.

For example, it means that we are no longer bound to the cycle of sin and guilt; God's power can set us free (Rom. 4:24–25). We are not locked in to the old way of life; God's power gives us hope for new life. "As Christ was raised from the dead by the glory of the Father, we too . . . walk in newness of life" (Rom. 6:4).

The resurrection means that our whole lives, even our bodies, have worth and dignity in the sight of God. One day our bodies will be raised in glory to reign with Jesus (1 Cor. 6:13–14; Phil. 3:21). No wonder Paul would gladly surrender his earthbound, deathbound gains for a personal relationship with the risen Jesus!

Second, Paul says, knowing Jesus means knowing someone who suffers. Who can fathom the suffering of Jesus? We know that Jesus offered himself, suffered for sins, and died once for all. The Just for the unjust "that he might bring us to God" (1 Peter 3:18; cf. Rom. 6:10; Heb. 7:27; 9:12). He died to make full and complete atonement for the sins of our fallen race. Nothing can be added; nothing need be repeated. Yet, where the finished atonement meets the unfinished task there continues to be the suffering involvement of the crucified and risen Christ Jesus. It isn't quite enough to say that Jesus came, suffered, and died for us, rose again, and now reigns on high. It must also be said that our Savior still suffers, for he bears the continuing burden of redeeming mankind. Our sins against his love inflict new wounds upon him. Years ago I memorized these lines from one of John Masefield's poems, in which a Quaker lass confronts the town bully:

> "Saul Kane," she said, "when next you drink,
> Do me the gentleness to think
> That every drop of drink accursed
> Makes Christ within you die of thirst,
> That every dirty word you say
> Is one more flint upon His way,
> Another thorn about His head,
> Another mock by where He tread,

    Another nail, another cross,
    All that you are is that Christ's loss."

Our interceding High Priest is "touched with the feeling of our infirmities" (Heb. 4:15 KJV). The One who died for us is the One who cares, loves, and suffers for us.

Claude Thompson says that in the cross we see God's intention to plumb the depths of every iniquitous crevice in the universe; that means Jesus is still present and suffering, wherever sin is found. Leslie Weatherhead pictures our Redeemer walking along the Via Dolorosa of our sin and shame, bearing the burden none of us could carry. No wonder there is joy among the angels for every sinner who repents! The Christ we know is the Christ who yet suffers.

Christians are called to share Christ's suffering. In 2 Corinthians 1:5, Paul says that "we share abundantly in Christ's sufferings." He tells the Colossians that he rejoices in his sufferings to "complete what is lacking in Christ's afflictions for the sake of his body, that is, the church" (Col. 1:24). If we know Jesus, we share not only his power and victory, but also his hurt, pain, loss, and suffering.

To know Christ—to share resurrection life in Christ—puts us where he is. It places us in an attitude toward the world that evokes contradiction, reproach, and persecution. It leads us to share the awful pain of the world's sin. That is the double-edged sword piercing the heart of Jesus: he bears the world's rejection, yet bears without rejection the suffering of the world.

I think this is what Jesus means when he summons us to take up our cross and follow him. If we take Jesus seriously, his Spirit will awaken within us his own way of feeling and thinking about the world. We cannot follow him without becoming personally involved in his involvement with the sin and suffering of mankind.

Whoever said that knowing Jesus means that we will have health and wealth and happiness? Wherever did we learn that our Christian calling is to make money and have a good and easy life? We assume it is the chief business of religion to help us avoid suffering. But we did not learn that from either Jesus or his disciples.

Nor do we read it in Paul's letters. His care for the churches was such that he could say, "My little children, with whom I am again in travail until Christ be formed in you . . . " (Gal. 4:19).

We are affected by the persons we know. We are, then, affected by the suffering Jesus. We cannot live as though he did not suffer and call us to share suffering with him. The power of his resurrection is released in us for this purpose—to enable us to share his love with the world and to bear the inevitable suffering it brings.

Third, Paul says that knowing Jesus means knowing someone who died. Jesus came into our world to do the will of his Father. He was so fully committed to that mission that everything was valued or disvalued, grasped or thrown away, received or rejected, only in relation to it. In full obedience and total trust in his Father, he walked through the falsehoods and compromises of his society—straight to the cross, where he died.

The world knows very well how to deal with someone like Jesus. His sincerity was terrible. His integrity was intolerable. His purity was unbearable. So his countrymen hanged him on a cross outside the city gates. We are so familiar with the story that we easily forget this plain truth: *The life and teachings of Jesus were so incongruous with the way things were in his world that he had to die.* Yet he went willingly to that death because he supremely desired to do the will of his Father.

In Romans 6:5, Paul says that "we have been united with him in a death like his." In Galatians 2:20, "I have been crucified with Christ." And in Galatians 6:14, he says that he is so conscious of the cross that "the world has been crucified to me, and I to the world." These are stark affirmations.

"Becoming like him in his death" does not necessarily mean that we must die the way Jesus died. I do not believe Paul expected to go to a cross as a martyr, imitative of Jesus. But he reminded his Christian friends that he was "always carrying in the body the death of Jesus" (2 Cor. 4:10). As Karl Barth puts it, the dying of

Jesus was always present in Paul's living apostleship, which was "clothed with the shame of Christ's death," not with earthly honor.

Paul spoke in Philippians 2 of Christ's relinquishment of all claim to honor. Becoming like Christ, then, means relinquishing our claim to all earthly dependencies. These lines of Augustus Toplady are daily owned by everyone who has been raised with Christ and who lives in the power of his resurrection:

> In my hand no price I bring,
> Simply to thy cross I cling.

Paul strives "that I may know . . . the power of his resurrection, and may share his sufferings, becoming like him in his death" (v. 10). At first glance, the order in which Paul speaks of resurrection, suffering, and death is surprising. His order, however, is not accidental. Paul is not trying to change the Christian calendar and put Easter before Good Friday. He places *resurrection* first because he first met Jesus as the risen Lord—even as we meet him. Only in the power of the resurrection was Paul able to share the *sufferings* of Jesus. Apart from the resurrection, shared suffering is only shared pain; but in the resurrection, it becomes a healing force in our lives. "For as we share abundantly in Christ's sufferings, so through Christ we share abundantly in comfort too" (2 Cor. 1:5).

And finally, as Paul shared Christ's resurrection power, he was made to conform to his *death*. The Christian paradox is that life is found in death. At the cross, where we say yes to Jesus' way of expressing love, we experience the renewed life of his resurrection. At the cross, where we say yes to the death of our own self-sovereignty, we find the power of the risen Christ released in us. I wonder if we can ever learn it: The power that raised Jesus from the dead is effective through our dependency upon him. We cannot be raised through our own strength or self-confidence. If God redeemed the world through the shameful death of Christ, let us not think we can participate in that redemptive task by our own accomplishments.

Paul's first word in verse 10 is the *resurrection* of Christ and his experience of its power; the last word is his own *death*, which allows God to accomplish his resurrection. Resurrection power to resurrection hope—that is the Christian sequence.

If there is no final resurrection, no final consummation, we have no real hope. The resurrection of Christ demonstrates that the whole process of human life is going somewhere; there is meaning in our lives because God is in charge here. We live in the context of Christ's final victory—a victory we may now share in our suffering with Christ and our dying with him.

As Christians, we can say two things in response to Paul's declaration in Philippians 3. First, we too know Jesus. That is no claim of achievement, but an honest testimony that we now enjoy a personal relationship with him. Second, we do not know Jesus at all. The shallowness of our relationship with him is appalling. After all this time, we should know him far better! I once memorized some lines that describe us:

> Little keys, little keys,
> That unlock the little doors,
> That open them to little pains
> And little pleasures
> That divine so little
> And reveal so little;
> And yet, here, beyond,
> The great doors and the great locks,
> The giant doors and the giant locks,
> That the little keys will not unlock.

Before us are the giant doors that open to the great depths and riches of the knowledge of Christ Jesus. We stand before them, clutching our little keys.

The end is not yet. Our relationship with Christ is not all it could be. It is not all that it will be by his grace. But such as we have is real, authentic, unique, and precious to such a degree that nothing in all the world can match it.

● Discussion Questions

1. In your own words, answer the question, What does it mean to know Jesus?
2. How do you respond to the idea that the personhood of God is the ground of understanding our own personhood?
3. Do you agree that we come to know God in Jesus the same way we come to know other people? What does the divine-human relationship have in common with human relationships?
4. I have expressed concern that we let other Christians determine the ideal Christian life for us. How can we avoid such conformity? I do not mean that we can ignore the Bible, the church, and the proven truths of our faith. How do these influence our Christian life?
5. What difference does Jesus' resurrection make in your life? What difference should it make?
6. What are some ways we can share the sufferings of Jesus?
7. What must die in us if we are to conform to the death of Jesus?
8. I said that the shallowness of our relationship with Jesus is appalling. Do you agree? What keeps us from deeper relationship with him?
9. How do the rituals and traditions of the church help us in "knowing Jesus"? How do they hinder us?

C H A P T E R · 10
The Upward Call

Not that I have already obtained this or am already perfect; but I press on to make it my own, because Christ Jesus has made me his own. Brethren, I do not consider that I have made it my own; but one thing I do, forgetting what lies behind and straining forward to what lies ahead, I press on toward the goal for the prize of the upward call of God in Christ Jesus. Let those of us who are mature be thus minded; and if in anything you are otherwise minded, God will reveal that also to you. Only let us hold true to what we have attained (Phil. 3:12–16).

● In the verses we discussed in the previous chapter, Paul spoke confidently about knowing Jesus; his meeting with Christ on the Damascus road (Acts 9:1–19) was not just a brief encounter, but the start of a lasting relationship, personal and unique. That relationship put him in touch with the power of the resurrection. Knowing Jesus meant being involved with him in suffering; it meant identifying with him in his death. Over all of Paul's life was the reality of Christ's ultimate victory, the final triumph of the resurrection. That was the great hope and aspiration of the apostle, and it is the hope of all who share his faith in Christ. We live

> In hope that sends its shining ray
> Far down the future's broadening way.

These words of Washington Gladden's hymn express the reality that resurrection hope is not only something we hope to experience at the end of our earthly journey; it is also the reality ("the shining ray") that illuminates our interim pilgrimage.

This was the fundamental perspective of Paul's theology. (Theologians call it the *eschatological* perspective.) Paul understood the church to be a community formed and defined by the coming of Christ. His coming is the sign of the end of the old era and the coming of the last age, the kingdom of God. The Christian community is to live in the new age, by the power of the new age, which is the Holy Spirit. The church's formation, continuance, purpose, and life are determined by the call of Christ. Christians live in the confidence that the new age of the kingdom, inaugurated by the first coming of Christ, will be consummated in his second coming.

The church then lives "between the times." It lives in the world under the conditions existing in the present, passing age; yet it lives in the certain hope of this world's consummation. That hope, that consciousness of ultimate victory, puts the church in a posture of both confidence and conflict, both assurance and struggle.

● The Perfection to Come

This perspective is evident in Paul's words of Philippians 3, especially as he begins verse 12. His knowledge of Jesus Christ as his Lord puts Paul over against the goals and values of the present age. The things that would have been so significant to him before Christ are seen to have no purpose and no place in his world, because the new kingdom age has come. His life in the present world is lived in terms of his ultimate loyalty or "citizenship in heaven" (3:20 NIV). Paul knows Christ and shares his resurrection power. Still, he lives in the world; he has not attained the full life of the resurrection nor is he perfected.

Paul's emphasis of this point may suggest that there were some people at Philippi, as there were in other early churches (2 Thess. 2:2; 2 Tim. 2:17–18), who believed that the final resurrection had already occurred. Christ had risen, they had risen with him, and they were now living the perfect life. They had "arrived." The perfect ones had no more spiritual struggle, no more failure, no more need for growth.

Over against their false perfectionism, Paul places his recognition of his own human limitation and his intense desire to reach what is yet ahead. Whatever other Christians may claim, Paul knows he is no perfect model of the Christian life. He finds himself caught in the tension between what he has already attained and what he yet strives for. He does not know all there is to know. Nor has he gained all there is to gain or experienced all there is to experience.

The word *perfect* is found in verses 12 and 15 of the KJV (the RSV has *perfect* in verse 12 and *mature* in verse 15). In the first instance, perfection is denied; in the second, it is affirmed. Paul says, "Not that I have already obtained this or am already perfect" (v. 12). He does not claim to have the kind of perfection that is possible only in the future at the final resurrection. Elsewhere Paul notes that what God had begun in the Christians' lives would be completed at the "day of Jesus Christ" (1:6). He is keenly aware of the riches of grace not yet known, the depths of love yet undiscovered.

The same attitude was expressed by Ignatius, bishop of Antioch, who was martyred about fifty years after Paul. He said, "I do not give you commands as if I were someone great, for though I am a prisoner for the Name, I am not yet perfect in Jesus Christ; for now I do not begin to be a disciple, and I speak to you as to my fellow learners" (Kirsopp Lake's translation). The old saint wrote this to the Ephesian church while in Smyrna, on his way to martyrdom!

Paul was in prison when he wrote to the Philippian church, his own martyrdom on the horizon. Yet, for all his years of service and leadership, for all his authority and experience, he would have none of the perfectionism that assumed an air of superior holiness, immune to the moral struggles and the spiritual aspirations of other believers. True perfection recognizes that total perfection is impossible for us in this world.

In verse 15, however, a kind of perfection is affirmed: "Let those of us who are mature ["perfect" KJV] be thus minded." Paul recognizes a real, though relative perfection that is, in Ralph Martin's apt phrase, "appropriate to our state as redeemed and sanctified believers."

Commenting on these verses, John Wesley said, "There is a difference between one that is perfect, and one that is perfected. The one is fitted for the race, v. 15; the other, ready to receive the prize."

Paul identifies himself with those who are fit for the race—those strong in faith, who are described as "the true circumcision, who worship God in spirit, and glory in Christ Jesus, and put no confidence in the flesh" (v. 3). He points out that those who who are perfect or mature will have a mind to press on for "the prize of the upward call of God in Christ Jesus" (v. 14).

• Why Press On?

There is a special motive behind Paul's "pressing on." He wants to appropriate that for which Christ appropriated him. In each of the New Testament's narratives of his conversion (Acts 9:1–19; 22:6–16; 26:12–18), we find that Paul was conscripted to service by the crucified, risen Jesus. "Christ Jesus has made me his own," Paul says. Behind the apostleship of Paul is the sovereign, mysterious call of God in Jesus. God was "pleased to reveal his Son" to Paul (Gal. 1:16), in order to call him to Christian service.

Who of us has not wondered at the mysterious work of God's grace in our behalf? We feel the upward call or the inward pull of divine love, an unsought longing for the holy life, and we say, "Why me?" We cannot answer that. We have only the growing certainty that behind our immediate call is an eternal calling to know Christ in "the power of his resurrection, and [to] share his sufferings, becoming like him in his death, that if possible [we] may attain the resurrection from the dead" (3:10–11).

Paul wanted to attain whatever Christ had in mind when he

conscripted him. He did not know at the beginning what his journey in Christ would entail. He was never given a map to follow; he never knew the next step he would need to take. He only knew that he was moving forward. He was ever reaching, ever dreaming and planning—never knowing ahead of time the turnings of the road. He was confident, however, that in his unknowing he was known of God; in his insecurity he was secure in Christ.

He gives us a rather vague description of the goal toward which he is pressing. He simply says it is "the prize of the upward call of God in Christ Jesus" (3:14). Today's English Version describes the prize as "God's call through Christ Jesus to the life above." So it would seem that the prize is not something—it is Someone. The prize is fullness of life in Christ, for whom Paul had already suffered the loss of all things. The apostle pressed toward full and perfect fellowship with the One who had been his companion all along his journey.

Significantly, Paul does not describe his goal as "making it to heaven" or receiving a golden crown. Even in 2 Timothy 4:8, where he specifically mentions a crown, he speaks only of the "crown of righteousness," the culmination of a life of right relationship with God. What Christians receive from Christ is *Christ himself.* The goal of our journey, the prize awaiting us, is the perfection of our fellowship with Christ himself.

● The Passion to Know Christ

As Paul pursues the goal of fully knowing Christ, he says, "one thing I do" (literally, "but one thing"). He has one pursuit, one passion, one aim—yet it is described in two dimensions. What is behind is forgotten; what is ahead is strained for.

"Forgetting what lies behind" is a familiar line. Some think Paul is referring to the old ego-centered package of his Jewish heritage and achievements, the things that he now considered refuse. Others think he refers to everything he must put behind as the race of spiritual growth progresses; he is a runner who does not count the laps completed, but the ones yet to be run.

What are we to forget as we "run with perseverance the race . . . set before us" (Heb. 12:1)? We can be sure that Paul does not advise us to erase our "memory bank." Memory is too vital to our spiritual life and worship for that. Paul himself had first put into writing the words of Jesus at the Last Supper, "Do this in remembrance of me" (1 Cor. 11:24).

We may better understand what Paul means by "forgetting" as we consider the Bible's emphasis on remembering. In the Bible, remembering is a dynamic calling of the past into the present, so that it affects the actions or perceptions of the present. "Do this in remembrance of me" does not mean "Don't forget that Jesus died." And "Remember the sabbath day to keep it holy" does not mean "Oh, I remember, it's Sunday!" Remembrance at the Lord's Supper brings into the present the reality of Jesus' atoning death, allowing us to participate in its saving benefits. The injunction to "remember the sabbath day, to keep it holy" (Exod. 20:8) calls us to observe the Sabbath and keep its requirements, not merely to think about it.

So what does the New Testament mean by "forgetting"? To forgive and forget is not to forgive and not ever remember that an offense occurred; rather, to forget is to deliberately keep the past in the past and not bring it up to affect the present situation. The past is regarded as having no bearing or influence on the present spiritual outlook or personal relationships. Forgetting means the release of the past into the past. It means having the freedom to move into God's future, unchained by past failures—and past successes.

Too many of us allow the shadows of yesterday's failures to darken our hopes for tomorrow. We let our past mistakes, sins, and guilts bind us. We remember them. We allow them to be destructively present with us, stifling any real effort toward growth.

But our remembrance of past successes can be just as destructive. The past is all some people ever talk or think about; they always interpret their present situation and future hope in terms of their past honors or achievements. An aging athlete surrounds himself with his pictures, ribbons, and trophies. A Christian preacher constantly retells the story of a marvelous conversion experience.

We need to release our past successes as much as our past failures.

Paul would say, "Let's do one thing! Let the past be past. Put it in God's hands—the good, the bad, and the indifferent—whatever is behind you. Let it go. God is calling you into the future."

Oddly enough, the right kind of remembering can help us achieve the right kind of forgetting. As we remember Jesus in the Lord's Supper, we are brought to the cross and the power of God's forgiving love. There we are released from the stifling guilt and regret of our sins. As we remember the Sabbath day, we are reminded of who we are as the redeemed people of God. We are set free from the tyranny of our frenzied secular culture. As we remember, we can forget, and we can go on.

The forgetting process involves the very act of reaching forward to what lies ahead. A famous sermon by Harry Emerson Fosdick was entitled, "The Expulsive Power of a New Affection." A new hope, a new vision, and a new love can free us from the past more decisively than trying to forget.

Paul describes his reaching for the future in vivid terms: "Straining forward . . . I press on." Strange that the apostle of grace, who put no confidence in works "lest any man should boast" (Eph. 2:9), should use the language of a straining runner, pushing on for the prize. Has Paul suddenly traded the truth of grace for the false gospel of works? Has he exchanged faith for effort?

Two comments may be in order. First, we should notice that Paul's efforts toward the goal are *response* efforts. He knows that God began the work in his life, and God will bring it to completion (1:6). He declares that God is working in the body of believers, willing and working for his good pleasure (2:13). So Paul puts no confidence in "the flesh," the self-motivated accomplishments of any Christian (3:3). He realizes that the whole process of salvation and spiritual growth rests on the divine initiative. He strains forward in response to the One who has laid hold of him, entrusted him with a vision, and called him to a task. He exercises faith by committing his total life and energy to God's work. For Paul, faith means far more than passive mental acceptance of the truth about Jesus Christ; it means entrusting one's whole self to him, making a total commitment of oneself to Christ.

Second, we should remember that Paul's goal inspired him to keep growing, reaching, gaining, and hoping. None of his struggles dimmed the vitality of his pursuit. None of his hardships quenched his desire for what was yet ahead for him in Christ.

Paul's words seem like the energetic declaration of a young man in the dawning years of a great career. It is remarkable that they come from an old man whose ministry is winding down—in prison.

I think of today's ministers who move toward retirement by securing their investments and emotionally disengaging from the ministerial round. Granted, we cannot neatly transpose Paul's situation into our own. But I'm afraid his passion to know Christ, his longing to know more of Christ, and his straining toward the goal are less observable among us.

What energized the apostle over his long and difficult years of ministry? Part of the answer can be found in the character of his call. He knew he had been called of God, as certainly as the Old Testament prophets did. That clear call sustained him.

Part of the answer, too, can be found in the character of Paul's vision of Christ. It filled his horizons. He saw Christ, knew Christ, loved Christ everywhere he went. He saw Christ in creation, knew him in redemption, loved him in daily personal fellowship, and claimed him as Lord of all his life. That vision of Jesus never dimmed; its glory never faded. Nothing less than the presence of Jesus himself could keep the apostle's hopes bright. Nothing else than the Spirit of Christ could vitalize and strengthen him through the long, hard missionary years.

• Being "Otherwise" Minded

Paul assumes that mature Christians will share his perspective and join him in the journey. But some may not see things his way. The apostle's own thinking had been radically altered because God had revealed his Son to him. So he says, "If in anything you are otherwise minded, God will reveal that also to you" (3:15). Paul could preach, teach, exhort, testify, and sometimes command; but he could not transform anyone's way of thinking. Only the illumination of the Spirit can do that. Only God can renew our minds.

And Paul knows that his own perspective is not the universal model. The center of the life of the Philippian church is the Lord, not the apostle. So the perspective that the Philippians are to have on the Christian life is determined by the Lord. Paul has a unique place in their affection as pastor and teacher, but they are not called to have the "mind" of Paul. Rather, they are expected to act on the "mind" that is theirs "in Christ Jesus" (2:5).

Paul's words raise a sensitive issue. Differing perspectives and conflicting viewpoints are held by Christians today. What are we to say of those who are "otherwise minded" than ourselves? The apostle's counsel is good for us: God is the revealer. While we may teach, preach, testify, exhort, and occasionally command, only God can make an "otherwise" mind otherwise!

His final word is crucial: "Only let us hold true to what we have attained" (3:16). That is, we need whatever it took to get us where we are if we are to go all the way with Christ. Whatever growth and transformation we need to experience will come about by the same faith, love, and obedience we had when we began the Christian journey.

Each denomination uses special terms to express the meaning of the gospel and to convey the nature of the Christian life. These terms are freighted with holy meaning. However, Christians in other denominations are "otherwise minded" and may not accept them. From someone's perspective, each of us is "otherwise minded"; and we place other Christians in that position. This is why Paul's word is so crucial. Before we begin discussion of our differences, Paul asks us, "What light do you have on the subject? Are you walking in it? By what means have you progressed on your journey of faith? Are you being true to them?"

Before we can reject the beliefs of others, we must consider whether we are being true to what we ourselves believe. It is easier to doubt than to trust, easier to criticize than obey. So Paul drives us back to the heart of the matter—obedient response to Christ.

The divisions within the Philippian church were not healed by total agreement, nor will those within the church today. The central, unifying reality among us is Jesus Christ the Lord, who calls us to himself.

God is the revealer of truth. He will make himself known to our "otherwise" minds. "But whatever be the point that we have already reached, let us persevere in the same course" (3:16 WEYMOUTH).

• Discussion Questions

1. Discuss what it means for the church to be a community of people living "between the times." How does this perspective help us understand that we are to be in the world and not of it?

2. The word *perfect* has many meanings. In what sense is a Christian perfect? In what respects is the Christian reaching toward perfection? What is the difference between a "perfect" heart and a "mature" heart?

3. I believe Paul was deeply conscious of having been "conscripted" for the Lord's work. Should we have anything like that same feeling about ourselves? Discuss.

4. Do you agree that Paul did not know where his spiritual journey would take him? Why or why not? Can we expect God to show us his plan for our lives? If not, can we find security in the fact that we have been grasped by God in Christ?

5. How would you describe the goal of Paul's life?

6. What do you think Paul means when he says we must "forget what is behind"?

7. Paul speaks of "straining" toward the goal of the Christian life. Do you think he is teaching a form of "salvation by works"?

8. I think Paul kept reaching out for more of Christ until the day he died; but I do not see much of this kind of hunger among Christians today. What do you think?

9. What should be our attitude toward Christians who differ—some seriously—with our point of view? Do you agree that we cannot change someone else's way of thinking? Discuss.

10. What do you think Paul means when he says we must hold true to what we have attained?

CHAPTER · 11

Rejoice in the Lord

Rejoice in the Lord always; again I will say, Rejoice. Let all men know your forbearance. The Lord is at hand. Have no anxiety about anything, but in everything by prayer and supplication with thanksgiving let your requests be made known to God. And the peace of God, which passes all understanding, will keep your hearts and your minds in Christ Jesus (Phil. 4:4–7).

● Paul tells the Philippians that the whole of life is to be lived "in the Lord." His imprisonment has made most of his brethren confident "in the Lord" (1:14), he hopes "in the Lord" to send Timothy to Philippi (2:19), and he trusts "in the Lord" that he will be able to come as well (2:24). The Philippians are to receive Epaphroditus "in the Lord" (2:29). He gives them a clear command: "Rejoice in the Lord" (3:1; 4:4). They are to "stand firm thus in the Lord" (4:1). Two women in their congregation are to "agree in the Lord" (4:2). And finally, Paul rejoices "in the Lord greatly" because the Philippians have renewed their care of him (4:10).

"In the Lord" is not a casual phrase. The earliest Christian creed was, "Jesus is Lord." The Christians used that declaration in their worship and witness to affirm their faith that Jesus, who "humbled himself and became obedient unto death, even death on a cross," had been highly exalted and given a name above every name, "that at the name of Jesus every knee should bow, in heaven and on earth and under the earth, and every tongue confess that Jesus Christ is Lord, to the glory of God the Father" (2:8–11).

Jesus' name signified his authority as the revealer of God and the mediator of salvation. The church worshiped him as the Lord of the universe, the cosmic Christ. They knew him as the Lord of history and of the church. He was present among them in the person of the Holy Spirit, whose outpouring on the church demonstrated Christ's continuing authority and power. At his coming at the end of the age, his lordship will be universally recognized. Then, all things will have been put "under his feet" and every tongue will confess that Jesus is Lord.

In the meantime, believers live "in the Lord." That is, they live in recognition of his sovereignty and in acceptance of his authority.

Christians live in fellowship with Jesus. They live in the power of the risen Master, who is Lord. Jesus is the center of life, and the Spirit—who testifies to his lordship—is the dynamic force of life "in the Lord." Christians believe the whole of life, not just its moral or religious aspects, is to be lived "in the Lord."

• Commanded to Rejoice

In this context we can best understand Paul's threefold command to "rejoice in the Lord." We are to have an attitude of continuing gladness and rejoicing in the Lord. Paul's word is an imperative, given in view of real church problems. How can he expect us to rejoice always?

A brief review of the epistle will clarify this. Two leading women who had worked with the apostles and other Christian leaders, perhaps even in establishing the church, are in a disagreement serious enough for Paul to mention them by name and to ask the church to help settle their dispute (4:2–3). Some people in the church are enemies of the cross—making the Christian claim, but not living it (3:17–19). Judaizers are a source of confusion and division in the church (3:2). Paul is concerned about the way Epaphroditus will be received (2:28–30).

The Philippians need encouragement not to be frightened by their opponents (1:28) and assurance that, though some are preaching because of envy and rivalry, the gospel is still being advanced among them (1:15–18). Only the mind of Christ can save them from division (2:5–8).

To this church—filled with trouble, uncertainty, and division—Paul writes an epistle of joy.

He expresses joy in their fellowship (1:4), joy in the preaching of Christ (1:18), and joy in their prayers for his deliverance (1:19). He commends their joy in the faith (1:25). They are to complete his joy by having the mind of Christ (2:2). Paul even has joy as he anticipates being poured out as a sacrificial offering on their behalf (2:17). The Philippians are his "joy and crown" (4:1), and he rejoices in their renewed care for him (4:10). So many problems—so much joy!

The church's problems are not suspended to give time for occasional joy. Neither is joy suspended while problems are dealt with. Joy and trouble are experienced together.

In a way, it is strange that joy should be such a dominant part of the Christian life. The Gospels tell us that Jesus wept, never that he laughed. He accomplished our salvation through suffering, agony, and death. His disciples were persecuted and martyred. We are called to have the mind of the One who humbled himself and became obedient, even when God required him to die on a cross.

That cross gives us our life perspective. In its light we see our own sin and are brought to repentance and confession. We see in sharp relief the fallenness of our world and its consequent pain and hurt. The Spirit of the suffering Christ sensitizes us to the oppression and unjust suffering of others.

That we should be thankful for love and saving grace, that we should stand in awe and wonder at divine majesty manifested in suffering love, that we should worship and adore and love and obey—of course! That we should ourselves become, for love of Christ, involved in care and suffering for others—oh, yes!

But then we are commanded to rejoice—and to rejoice again. We wonder, What is the source of joy for the Christian? Where does rejoicing fit into everything else we know about the Jesus way of life?

• The Source of Divine Joy

I believe this joy began in the very nature of the triune God— Father, Son, and Holy Spirit. God's nature is to be a fellowship. Within God's own nature is continual giving and receiving, loving and sharing—and joy.

The creation itself reflects the joy in God. The psalms are full of the sounds of nature's praise to the Creator. The first human pair greet each other in joyful recognition. Throughout the Bible, the children of God are called to praise him and be joyful in him. Luke's account of the Son of God begins with the joy of his birth, records his joy in the midst of his ministry (10:21), and concludes with his disciples praising God in the temple.

Joy in the Lord is more than a capricious mood. It has a cause: the creature's response to the Creator, and the believer's response to the Savior.

Joy in the Lord seeks expression; it is a shared response to God. This is why joy is so often characteristic of the church's experience of worship. It explains why Paul makes so many references to joy as he describes his fellowship with the churches. Christians share the joy of Jesus' own communion with his Father and his obedience in doing the Father's will. These are at the heart of the Christian's joy.

Paul told the Galatians that joy was a fruit of the Spirit (5:22). He told the Romans that the kingdom of God is characterized by "righteousness and peace and joy in the Holy Spirit" (14:17). Such joy is present even in suffering; it cannot be nullified by death. This is because it does not depend upon outward circumstances or inward moods; it depends only upon God and our relationship with him through the Lord Jesus.

Rejoicing in the Lord is both a future hope and a present experience. It is a future hope because our present joy is always mixed with the sufferings of our human condition and with the anticipation of our final deliverance. We look forward to the return of Christ, when our joy will be perfect. Yet our present joy is real because we experience even now the fellowship of Christ through the Spirit. We live in the sure expectation of the victory he has already won.

A great reality undergirds our joy: The Lord in whom we rejoice "is at hand" (4:5). The Greek word Paul uses here literally means the Lord "is near," and it can refer either to nearness of place or to nearness in time. This is Paul's fifth reference in this brief letter to the coming of Christ (see 1:6, 10; 3:11, 20). The Lord's coming is near, and the Lord himself is present among us. So we do not think that the Lord is "up there" and soon will come "down here" to take us "up there." *He is here,* and his coming will unveil his presence and lordship to the whole world.

Our hope for his soon coming is not simply hope that he will come and take us away. We have the sure knowledge that he is in charge here, and his power will ultimately subdue all things. He is our risen Christ Jesus, who is our Lord now, present with us in power.

● Live in Forbearance

Knowing this, we can rejoice despite the crises and anxieties of the interim; and we can live before others in *forbearance.* The Greek word here is not easy to translate. Some versions use words such as *considerateness, humility, reasonableness, courtesy,* and *magnanimity.* Luther understood the word to mean an attitude that is glad before the Lord and lenient with other men. Wesley interpreted it to mean a yielding, sweet temper, the result of joy in the Lord.

But how can we live in forbearance? The world is rushing out of control, and Christ's church is fragmented by a thousand divisions. How can we have a gentle, forbearing spirit at a time like this?

Since we know that Jesus is sovereign, we do not need to be

defensive about ourselves or his church. We can shun rigidity and self-righteousness. We can afford to be forbearing—that is, humble toward others. Yes, we are to criticize the destructive systems of the world and seek their conversion; yet we can do it in a spirit of humility, reasonableness, and magnanimity. As we take our stand, we can be forbearing and not overbearing.

Like many other words of Paul, *forbearance* probes our conscience. It requires us to be humble in our judgment of the clear injustices and inequities in the world's structures. It reminds us that we can be right in the wrong way. Our view of injustice may be accurate, while we ourselves are inaccurately perceived. So our attitude toward all people, in and out of the church, must be one of repentance and humility. We must be glad before God and lenient before men because the Lord is at hand.

• "Have No Anxiety"

Unless the Lord were near, we could not take seriously Paul's further command to "have no anxiety about anything" (4:6). Worrying belongs to human life. We are naturally concerned about ourselves and our future. But Paul pushes us to a new perspective on our worries. That new perspective, that new center of gravity, is God. His words parallel those of 1 Peter 5:7, which says, "Cast all your anxieties on him, for he cares about you."

Paul and Peter are not telling us that God will relieve our anxieties by granting our wishes. They promise that God will relieve us of *anxiety,* not that he will take away what we are anxious about.

I read last week of a lonely, anxious woman who learned this the hard way. A friend promised that if she would be "born again," Jesus would satisfy all her needs and give her a husband. She is now the leader of a new "Anonymous" group—organized to help other "born againers" recover from the unwitting deception of sincere people who believe God's remedy for all anxiety is the fulfillment of our needs.

Paul leads us in a different direction. He counsels us to disengage from our desires. We need to know that we cannot secure our lives by anxious care. The trouble is that our concern for the things of this world is really self-concern. We care about what we care about, we want what we want. And in our self-centered wanting, we fall victim to anxiety. Then we frantically try to find some way to get rid of anxiety!

Jesus said, "Seek first his kingdom and his righteousness, and all these things shall be yours as well" (Matt. 6:33). This is the paradox of the kingdom of God. Do we really care about our food, clothes, house, and job? Then we must seek first the kingdom of God! Do we really want to be free from fretful concern for these things? Then we must trust the Father's care! Do we really want to be set free from anxiety? Then with thankfulness we must "take it to the Lord in prayer."

The burdens and cares of our human existence are real; but so is our freedom from anxiety about these things. We can have this freedom when we recognize that "the Lord is at hand" and open our hearts to him in trust and thanksgiving.

● Prayer and Thanksgiving

The contrast Paul makes between anxiety and prayer could not be more radical: On the one hand, we are to have "no anxiety about anything"; on the other, we are to rejoice "in everything by prayer."

In verse 6, Paul uses three different words for prayer. *Prayer* refers to prayer of all kinds. *Supplication* emphasizes our sense of need and our desire to bring our petitions before God. *Requests* are specific petitions about specific needs. Taken together, these three words invite us to pray with faith and expectancy about everything. H. C. G. Moule says this verse beckons us to the "fullest and freest speaking to the Lord." Whatever the sources of our anxiety, we are to open them up before God in prayer.

A good example is found in the way Hezekiah opened up the

letter of Sennacherib and spread it before the Lord (2 Kings 19:14ff.; Isa. 37:14ff.). The letter threatened the destruction of Judah by the Assyrian nation. Hezekiah addressed God, who is above all kingdoms of the earth, and asked him to see what the pagan general had written. He prayed to the sovereign, all-knowing God as though he did not know what was going on.

I believe this is what Paul had in mind when he urged the Philippians to open up everything to God. It is the way Jesus instructed us to pray, coming to our heavenly Father as children, telling him all our needs and wants. *Everything* is to be opened to God in prayer—with thanksgiving.

Paul's phrase, "with thanksgiving," is not an added afterthought. Bible scholars say those words belong with each of the three terms Paul uses: Our prayer is made with thanksgiving, our supplication is in thanksgiving, and our requests are bathed in thanksgiving. Our attitude of thanksgiving recognizes that in our particular situation, with all its burdens and cares, Jesus is indeed sovereign and both "near in space and nigh in time." When we are anxious, we are looking out for ourselves. We try to discern the future and plan ahead. When we praise, we recognize God. We release him to act, while we are released from anxiety.

Finally, Paul says, we are guarded by his peace. Karl Barth says that when we keep our troubles to ourselves, shutting them off from God, we are unguarded and vulnerable to every kind of danger. But when we open them to God with thanksgiving, we are surrounded by God's peace.

We are to let the peace of God rule in our hearts (see Col. 3:15). His peace guards our hearts and minds in ways beyond our understanding. As Fred Craddock says, "God's peace is on duty" in our hearts. We may be at peace because the Lord is at hand.

• Discussion Questions

1. What do you think Paul is emphasizing by his repeated use of the phrase "in the Lord"?

2. We are commanded to rejoice, just as we are commanded to love. How can rejoicing be commanded? How would you begin to obey the command?

3. Clearly, joy and trouble are not opposites. What is the opposite of joy? How can we really rejoice in the midst of trouble?

4. I have suggested that joy has its ultimate source in the nature of God himself. We often think of God as holy love. Why do we not think of him as holy joy?

5. Check a concordance to see where the words *rejoice, rejoicing,* and *joy* appear in the New Testament. How should we express joy in worship?

6. The idea that "the Lord is at hand" indicates the nearness of the Lord in space and in time. How should our church life be affected by the fact that he is soon to come, but is already here?

7. Give some examples of how a Christian can be "forbearing." I have suggested that we should be forbearing because we are under the sovereign lordship of Jesus. We have more cause to be repentant than judgmental. Do you agree? Explain.

8. We cannot eliminate anxiety from our lives. How would you distinguish between appropriate and inappropriate anxiety for the Christian? Give examples.

9. One aspect of prayer that relieves anxiety is that it requires total openness to God. Do you think Hezekiah's prayer is a good example of this? Why should we tell the all-knowing God what he already knows?

10. Why is thanksgiving an important part of prayer?

11. Karl Barth says that when we are not open to God, we are vulnerable to all kinds of danger. What dangers come to mind?

12. Is there a difference between (a) having the peace of God guard our hearts and minds, and (b) having peace of mind? Discuss.

CHAPTER · 12

On Thinking and Doing

Finally, brethren, whatever is true, whatever is honorable, whatever is just, whatever is pure, whatever is lovely, whatever is gracious, if there is any excellence, if there is anything worthy of praise, think about these things. What you have learned and received and heard and seen in me, do; and the God of peace will be with you (Phil. 4:8–9).

● After all he has said about Jesus and the life we have in him, it may seem strange for Paul to say, "Now I have a list of some good things you need to keep in mind." Especially when the things he lists are not specifically Christian virtues.

Both Jewish and Gentile philosophers commonly gave their students lists of virtues to cultivate and vices to avoid. Such lists probably were used in the synagogues and schools Paul had attended. In his other writings, Paul made lists of vices that Christians should avoid (Rom. 1:29–31; 1 Cor. 6:9–10; Gal. 5:19–21); but nowhere else does he furnish a list of general virtues. So why do it here?

Perhaps he felt that his reassuring words should be buttressed by the instructive words of positive thought and action. Some Bible scholars think he was responding to questions the Philippians had asked about Christian ethics.

In any case, these words are not mere afterthoughts. They are not just an exhortation to positive thinking. Paul did not write this epistle to help his Christian friends think noble thoughts about noble things. On the other hand, the proverb is true, "As [a man] thinketh in his heart, so is he" (Prov. 23:7 KJV). We are what we think.

Jesus said that the vacuum of a newly converted life may draw to itself more evil spirits than inhabited it before (Matt. 12:43–45). So it is not enough to be clean; we must be filled. And what we are filled with is as significant as what we are cleansed of. "Whatever is true, whatever is honorable, whatever is just, whatever is pure, whatever is lovely, whatever is gracious"—these are thoughts to fill us and truths to guide us.

• Common Virtues or Christian Virtues?

The virtues Paul mentions are the same ones the people of God have loved and lived by through the long years of salvation history. They do not belong only to Christians, nor does one have to be a special sort of person to achieve them. They are the common virtues extolled by the teachers of morality in the pagan world. Paul picked them out of the vocabulary of that world, held them up before the Philippians (and before us all), and said, "Here— reckon with these."

We need to realize that the world knows what is good. We must face the fact that some people in the world have more basic ethical integrity than we Christians have. That can be a source of embarrassment.

It ought just as well to be a source of celebration, for it underscores the fact that all mankind is made in the image of God. The "Word made flesh" shines to some degree in the life of every person in the world. All mankind lives and moves and has its being in Christ (Acts 17:28). So there is goodness in the world, fallen though it is, because God has left himself a witness here (Acts 14:17).

The goodness that the world knows is not much different from the goodness that the Christian knows. In fact, there are not strictly Christian morals. Christian morality is unique, to be sure;

but its uniqueness is not to be found in its moral content. Actually, our Christian morals are universal because they are grounded in God. They are the morals most persons hold, whether or not they act according to them.

When a well-known religious figure falls into immorality or fraud, the world rises up to cry, "Hypocrite!" The world knows how a Christian ought to act because it knows how all people ought to act. In that sense, our morals are not uniquely Christian.

We may affirm and celebrate the ethical standards of the world because they testify to the prevenient grace of our creator-redeemer God.

Some individuals deny this. They believe that the only source of truth is the Bible. So they discount or reject the value of any morality that is not derived from Scripture. But if we believe in one God, "the Father almighty, maker of heaven and earth," incarnate in the One who is the truth, then we know that he must be the source of all truth—however it may be distorted by ignorance. He is also the source of all morality, however degraded by sin.

This does not mean that we should consider the world's morality to be sufficient; nor does it mean that we should compromise with it. We know that God has uniquely revealed himself in Jesus our Lord. He is "the way, and the truth, and the life" (John 14:6). "And we know that the Son of God has come and has given us understanding, to know him who is true; and we are in him who is true, in his son Jesus Christ. This is the true God and eternal life" (1 John 5:20).

● "Think About These Things"

Let's look at Paul's familiar virtues one by one. This will give us a clearer understanding of how unique they are.

"Whatever is true." This phrase takes us out of the realm of false emotion and brings us into reality. We know that we are to be people who love the truth; but we wish the apostle had given us

more help to discern the truth in our culture. It is not easy to find truth in speech, in thought, in attitude, and in action. Where shall we find it?

The sounds of the world surround us. But the ornithologist hears the songbird; the mother hears her baby's cry; and the child of God listens for the ring of truth. Though it may be difficult to discern, truth attracts us.

"Whatever is honorable." Indeed the honorable things of this world are worthy of reverence. We know that God alone is to be worshiped; but in "awesome wonder" we contemplate the world his hands have made. In his creatures we see his reflected grandeur; we perceive his nobility. A desire deep within us says, "Hold it. Treasure it. It is the image of God."

"Whatever is just." This phrase calls us to rightness of relationships. *Just* is Paul's most common term for righteousness, and it simply means whatever is right in our dealings and behaviors. So much is wrong. Our passion is for the right. Jesus said, "Blessed are those who hunger and thirst for righteousness, for they shall be satisfied" (Matt. 5:6).

"Whatever is pure." We customarily use *pure* to refer to sexual and moral purity; but it is a comprehensive term that applies to all of life. We live in a world of mixed motives, rationalized behavior, compromised relationships, and clouded vision. "Whatever is pure" is unmixed. And the pure in heart see God.

"Whatever is lovely." Lovely things attract people, are winsome, and inspire love. A lovely thing is worthy of being loved. Anything that is attractive but evil cannot be *lovely* in the way Paul uses the word. But whatever is attractive because it is beautiful and good, whatever is charming because it is godly and pure, is lovely.

"Whatever is gracious." Moffatt translates this as "high toned"; other translators use the phrase "of good report." When we observe someone engaging in a gracious, generous act, we say, "That speaks well of them." We pause and reflect on their behavior, and thus are drawn toward God.

Paul's last phrase is expansive: *"If there is any excellence, if there is anything worthy of praise. . . . "* Paul opens his arms to the world and says, "Whatever is excellent out there—whatever is praise-worthy out there—we ought to take into account." The people of God cannot ignore what the rest of the world esteems to be good. We must meditate on it, seek to understand it, and learn whether it indeed reveals anything about our relationship with God.

An able theologian and Bible scholar, John Wesley also studied medicine, mathematics, logic, science, and literature. He left at the City Road Chapel an edition of Shakespeare's works annotated in his own hand; but one of his successors burned it as something "which tended not to edification." I wonder if we are just as blind to what we might learn from the culture of our own day. Whatever has merit for the rest of society has some merit for us.

Our society's best virtues are not necessarily our virtues as Christians. However, we must recognize that our society's virtues often reflect the image of God and reveal the grace of God. We are not blind to the evil of the world; rather, our eyes are open to the good working of our redeeming God, "for from him and through him and to him are all things. To him be glory for ever" (Rom. 11:36).

All these things we are to think about. The Greek word Paul uses for *think* literally means we are to "take into account" or "reckon." We reckon with the weather on our plans, reckon with the fact of taxes, and reckon with the law of gravity. These things are taken into account in the ordering of our lives, given weight in our decisions. Paul makes an appeal for discerning moral judgment in a world of disvalue, unrealities, and deceits. The degree to which we succumb to shoddy thinking, careless behavior, and destructive attitudes is the degree to which we fall into the ways of the world. Paul tells us to live by the values that are real. He calls us to pursue the truth, respect what is honorable, make decisions in the interest of justice, seek purity in our behavior, and respond gratefully to what is lovely and gracious.

John Bunyan understood the importance of such a life. In *The Pilgrim's Progress* he portrays an old man bent over a muck rake as he turns over a mound of trash and filth, looking for some gold. Meanwhile a bright angel on celestial wings is hovering over him with a crown of gold, ready to place it on his head if he will only straighten up.

The point has been emphasized that the things Paul tells the Philippians to think about and reckon on are not uniquely Christian virtues. They come from the common stock of moral values that were present in the first-century world. So what gives them any special significance in the lives of Christians? What makes them anything more than good advice of the same sort that is handed out to the young by the people of the world? If they are, after all, "worldly virtues," what place do they have in the Word of God and what sort of authority do they have over us?

Simply put, what makes them different for us is Jesus. He is the One who makes the difference for us in everything. We cannot understand Paul's exhortations and seek to live by them without the power of Jesus. These virtues are embodied in him. He gives eternal meaning to them. He defines them for us—that is, he lives them out in his own life, and we see them in action there.

If we see truth in the world and celebrate it, we celebrate the presence of the One who said, "I am the truth."

We see honor in all kinds of activity in the world: the honor of rulers who oppress the poor, the honor of learned scholars who are proud and petty, even the honor among thieves. But when we see the way Jesus walks among us—with dignity and simplicity, with poise and grace—our eyes are opened to recognize true honor and to want it.

The poor and the oppressed recognize justice in him. They see that what he does is right; he always makes things and persons right. Even many who are not Christians themselves, when confronted with a moral dilemma, might ask themselves, "What would Jesus do?"

The world has so defiled the idea of purity that only eyes cleansed by a vision of Jesus can still perceive it. We know what purity is when we observe his singleness of heart toward his heavenly Father, his obedience to his Father's will, and the integrity of his character and ministry.

So it is with each of the virtues that Paul enumerates. They have unique meaning for the Christian because of Jesus Christ. When we say "truth" or "honor" or "purity," we think *Jesus*. His life displays for us the meaning of these things we are to think about.

He is more than our example in these things; he is our strength. The Spirit of Jesus is the dynamic force that brings about any actual change in our lives as we reckon with truth, honor, justice, and all of the other virtues. This is what keeps them from being mere advices.

When Paul holds up these virtues before the Philippians, he does not say, "Here are your ideals. Now work as hard as you can to achieve them. These are the best virtues of the world; but you can outshine the world in living up to these ideals if you try." Instead, he emphasizes that underneath these virtues is the presence of Jesus. He reminds them that, as they "think about these things," they are to have the mind of Christ Jesus (2:5) and share the transforming presence of his Spirit.

● **Express the Truth in Your Life**

Now Paul moves in a different direction. He holds up before the Philippians what he has taught them and how he has lived before them, and he says, "Do these things" (v. 9). This is characteristic of biblical faith. The believer's contemplation of truth must always lead to an expression of that truth in his life.

The Philippian letter is a dynamic mixture of truth and life. Christian witness and insight are to be tied to practical daily actions. The Christians' lives are to be shared, side by side, in one spirit and one mind (1:27-28). The great hymn of Christ's self-emptying and lordship is to express their attitude toward one another (2:1-11). They are to shine as lights in the world, which means they don't grumble or complain (2:14).

"What you have learned and received and heard and seen in me, do; and the God of peace will be with you" (4:9). Let's take a closer look at the key words of this verse:

Learned is our translation of a Greek word that is rooted in the word meaning *disciple*. The apostle-teacher reminds the Philippians that he has discipled them; he has taught them a way of life, not merely given them some interesting ideas.

Received is the same word Paul uses in 1 Corinthians 11:23, "I received from the Lord what I also delivered to you. . . . " He had not given the Philippians some new revelation or novel interpretation of Jesus' teaching. It was the common stock of apostolic preaching, shared by all the disciples of the Lord.

Heard and seen is a phrase that makes us think of the words of 1 John concerning the incarnate Jesus, "That which we have seen and heard we proclaim also to you, so that you may have fellowship with us" (1:3). First John declares that Jesus had lived before the Christians; he could be seen and heard and touched. Likewise, here in Philippians, Paul declares that he had lived in the church's presence. He offers his own behavior to them as an example of life in Christ.

We are accustomed to at least a little more humility than Paul seems to manifest here. Why does he so forthrightly point to his own life as an example for other Christians?

Paul's vocation as an apostle involved the task of *living* the gospel as well as proclaiming it. His very life was a testimony to the truth of what he preached. The integrity of his gospel message was tied to the integrity of his life. He did not claim to be a "perfect specimen" of a Christian, as he clearly confessed in 3:12. But he lived in grace, reaching forward and growing. The honesty and transparency of his life testified to the integrity of the gospel he preached. So it was with all the apostles; their lives bore witness to the reality of their message about Jesus Christ. In fact, their lives were part of the message itself.

Early Christians had no New Testament as we do, nor did they have the church customs many of us have. We have a general understanding of how the Christian life ought to be lived. We have our own denominational traditions, which include lifestyle expectations, personal disciplines, and guidelines for group behavior. We have available thousands of books and pamphlets that instruct us in the Christian life. But what did the Christians of Paul's time have to guide them?

Jewish converts had the Old Testament, as did Gentiles who had been attracted to the Jewish synagogues. But pagan Gentile converts had only the message of the apostles, the stories that other Christians told about Jesus, a few apostolic letters to the churches, and—the lives of the apostles. So how were they to act? What did it mean to follow Jesus Christ and belong to the fellowship of Christian believers? There in their presence, living before them, were models of the gospel. The apostles were examples of love and forgiveness, living witnesses to what the Christian life was all about.

So Paul did not point to himself in pride and say, "Look at me!" But he was compelled to say, "Be imitators of me, as I am of Christ" (1 Cor. 11:1).

These are things to reckon with. We have much thinking to do; but we also have much *doing* to do! Part of the problem with discussing the Christian virtues is that, when we understand them, we suppose we have made them our own. But the apostle's command to *do* is as strong as his command to think.

The Christian life is not a set of rules to be followed; it is a new life that can be demonstrated only in living persons. That was true of the Philippians, who had little to read about the Christian life; it is still true for us, who may have read too much about it.

The final revelation of the gospel is not a list of commands, laws, or rules—it is a person, Jesus the Christ, who lived among us and embodied the character of God. Paul understood that his own life among other Christians embodied his relationship with Christ and so became a legitimate guide for their living.

We should understand, too, that our lives are in view. We are displaying the gospel to the world around us. It is a world that still understands the meaning of the gospel by what it sees in the lives of those who claim to follow Christ. We do not boast to our neighbors, saying, "You ought to be like me." Yet the gospel is really learned in someone's life. What is received of the truth comes through someone; what is heard from God is heard from someone; and what is seen of the gospel is seen in someone.

Implicit in our lives, then, is the invitation, "Be ye followers of me, even as I also am of Christ" (1 Cor. 11:1 KJV).

• Discussion Questions

1. Why do you think Paul includes a list of virtues that are actually virtues of the world?
2. Is it true that we are what we think? (See Prov. 4:23 and Matt. 12:34.) Discuss.
3. I think we seldom guard what we see and hear; and we seldom deliberately choose to think about what is true, just, and lovely. Do you agree? If so, why do you suppose we act this way?
4. How do you explain the fact that some non-Christians seem to have higher ethical standards than Christians?
5. Do you agree that the goodness of the world testifies to its creation by God, and that the goodness of persons testify to the image of God within them? Discuss.
6. Is the world's standard of goodness pretty much the same as a Christian's standard of goodness? If not, how do they differ?
7. I believe it is very hard to discern the truth in what we see and hear, and difficult to speak the truth accurately. What do you think of this?
8. How would you summarize the list of virtues that Paul gives in Philippians 4:8–9? Try to put them in your own words, not using the biblical terms.
9. Paul does not give us specific instructions on how we are to think about the things he mentions. In practical terms, what are some ways we can do this?
10. How do you respond to the idea that Jesus makes Christian ethics different from ethics in general? Give an example of this.
11. Should we be able to say, "What you have heard from me and seen in my life, do it"? How is Paul's relationship with the Philippian church different from our relationship with those around us?

CHAPTER · 13

The Open Secret of Strength

I rejoice in the Lord greatly that now at length you have revived your concern for me; you were indeed concerned for me, but you had no opportunity. Not that I complain of want; for I have learned, in whatever state I am, to be content. I know how to be abased, and I know how to abound; in any and all circumstances I have learned the secret of facing plenty and hunger, abundance and want. I can do all things in him who strengthens me (Phil. 4:10–13).

● The apostle Paul is in prison. Some of the preachers who have taken his place are not sincere (1:17). He doesn't know if he will live or die (1:20; 2:23). He has "suffered the loss of all things" (3:8). Yet he has the audacity to declare, "I can do all things in him who strengthens me."

This helpless man in prison is asserting his independence. How can it be?

He says, "I have learned . . . to be content." Sounds like something a self-sufficient person might say. Paul is not self-sufficient; but he has learned the secret of facing plenty or hunger, abundance or want, with the same confident outlook.

The contradictions are amazing. He possesses nothing, but he has no wants. His future is uncertain, but he is content. He has experienced wealth and poverty, exaltation and humiliation, fullness and emptiness. Now he is a prisoner, yet he declares, "I can do all things. . . . " And, for that matter, his declaration made no change in his situation. It was not the prelude to freedom; it did not signal the end of want or hunger or humiliation. Yet it stands: "I can do all things in him who strengthens me." A person who can say such things must be privy to a secret, a wonderful secret of strength.

We need to learn that secret for we, too, face the changing fortunes of success and failure, joy and sorrow, clarity and mystery. We must be strong to endure temptation, make tough decisions, weather the crisis, and handle the success. Are you about to encounter a situation for which you need to be strong? Then take heart. There is a secret of strength. Like the gospel itself, it is an open secret. Paul learned it, and in these closing verses of Philippians he tells us what it is:

In his inadequacy he was adequate,
In his dependency he was independent,
Because he was totally dependent
On the One who was totally adequate.

The secret of strength is total dependency on Christ. Paul's declaration, "I can do all things," can never stand alone because its validity rests on the last phrase, "in him who strengthens me."

• Strong Christians or Strong Individuals?

The secret of strength is not a strong personality. Paul does not say, "I am strong." Instead, he says, "When I am weak, then I am strong" (2 Cor. 12:10). Most of us would say that when we are strong we feel weak enough; but when we are weak—Lord, have mercy! In feeling that way, we illustrate our tendency to base our spiritual strength on personal strength.

Paul was making a statement about Christ, not about himself. He did not say that he had the endurance and stamina to see his situation through. To be sure, he was a strong person with a bold personality. (Timothy could probably vouch for that—as could Barnabas, Peter, and Mark!) Paul was a strong person; yet he never spoke of his personal strength. He spoke instead of his weakness and his total dependence upon Christ.

Strong Christians are not necessarily strong persons. They are real persons who have discovered they have no strength in themselves, so have submitted their weakness to Jesus. In him they have found the strength that is inexhaustible.

We tend to think that Christians with strong personalities are bound to be spiritually strong. They are the survivors. They can cope. They are flexible. They have emotional stamina to handle stress and pressure. They recover from sickness and loss with increased vision and purpose. They are the constitutionally strong. (May their tribe increase!)

But other Christians are naturally weak and fragile. They do not have aggressive personalities, and they are low on emotional energy. They must be careful to avoid overload and overextension. They need plenty of peace and quiet. (May their tribe increase as well!)

Let us not confuse personal strength with spiritual strength, nor a fragile personality with frail spirituality. We will misjudge others—and misjudge ourselves—if we do this.

Nor is the secret of spiritual strength analogous to the secret of physical strength. We know how to build muscles. We begin slowly, exercise regularly, and so begin to enlarge lung capacity and strengthen the heart. First we lift the light weights, then the springs and pulleys, and then the heavy weights. "No pain, no gain"—that's how muscles grow. Time and perseverance, sweat and strain, always produce results.

Is that how it is with spiritual strength? Do we begin small, believing God for something believable, praying for something manageable, and gradually working up to something wonderful?

Do we pray for little things and work our way up to bold claims? Do we begin praying about a cold and work up to praying for the healing of cancer?

No. The truth is, we never become strong in faith as we become strong in body. We do not have "faith muscles" to develop through exercise, because our strength is never in ourselves.

We say to a new Christian, "Depend on Jesus. Don't depend on your own strength. Trust him every day—every hour—every moment of the day. Stay close to him and trust him." But we don't say that to a more mature Christian. We suppose that, as we become older Christians, we do not have to depend upon him quite so much as when we were young and weak in faith.

We have heard much about great men and women of prayer and great heroes of the faith. I wonder, is a person a "great person of prayer" when he or she isn't praying? Is a "hero of the faith" still strong in faith when he or she is doubtful and troubled? This isn't to deny the value of years of faithful praying and trusting God. But my point is this: Faith is not something we have; power in prayer is not something we carry around like enlarged biceps. Spiritual strength is not something we have. *We never become spiritually strong.* Jesus is always our strength.

• Self-Dependency vs. Christ-Dependency

Of course, there are benefits of being strong. But the problem with strength is that it leads to self-dependency.

We are proud of our abilities to plan, work, and get the job done. And we ask for the Lord's help all along the way. He becomes the "giver of extra strength" for the tasks we have assigned to ourselves. We thus bring him into the system we have established and ask him to help us accomplish the goals we have set. We do all we can and trust God to make up our deficit. We say to one another, "Just do your best. That is all God expects of us."

Our Christian living has become something that we offer to God. It is an achievement or performance—done with his help, of course—by which we seek to gain his approval or demonstrate our commitment to him. But nothing we do is ever quite enough. And how do we know when we have done our best?

Some talented athletes have reached goals that have earned them bronze medals. That medal symbolizes both an achievement and a question: "Did I really do my best?" Others have earned medals of silver. They still have a haunting doubt: "Could I have done more?" Only a few have reached the top of achievement, and their medals are gold. Yet their question is the same: "Could I have done any better?" In the arena of human competition, no achievement is ever quite enough. Another goal always lies ahead, challenging us to more effort, more discipline, and more achievement.

When we view the spiritual life in this way, the strong rise to the challenge while the weak fall behind, guilty and discouraged.

When we say, "Do all you can, and God will step in to make up the rest," we picture God as the Lord of the gaps. We regard him as the One who compensates for our lack of ability.

Two conversations—one a long time ago and another quite recent—have deeply influenced my thinking about this.

While I was a college chaplain, a pre-med student married a beautiful young woman. When he entered medical school, he became absorbed in his studies and filled with the vision of great things he would do for God. The couple lived in a dingy little apartment, and she found a job to help pay the bills. They were on their way. He was consumed with his work; she was bored and lonely. He came home one day to find the note, "Sorry, I have had it. Good-bye."

He was devastated. Suddenly, all the things he had taken for granted were crushed. He could see his failures to communicate with his wife and to give her loving support. He was beside himself with remorse. We spent some hours together, talking about his situation.

He said, "I know that as a Christian I ought to be able to handle this better. I ought to be able to trust God and cope with this. But I am so devastated that I don't even have the strength to believe."

His comment was a sudden insight to us both. His words almost hung in the air between us: *I don't even have the strength to believe.* Our common assumptions about trust in God were suddenly exposed. We had to think again about the meaning of faith. He had made his statement on the unexamined assumption that faith takes strength. Faith had become a subtle form of works, which he could not now perform. He had accepted a gospel for the strong. And when he needed faith the most, this young man was least able to exercise it.

Must we be strong to have faith? If so, when life falls apart and its values are destroyed, where will we find the strength to survive? In such a situation, our distorted gospel is not good news at all; it is good advice to the strong and condemnation to the weak.

More recently, a friend said to me from his hospital bed, "I sure am glad I was prayed up before I came to this place. I've been so sick I haven't even had the strength to pray." Again I saw the same religious perception: We need strength to pray and believe God.

Was my friend really saying that we had better keep praying when we are well and strong, because the time may come when we are sick, and we will need all those stored-up prayers to tide us over? If that is the case, we should attend all the prayer meetings we can. We should keep our spiritual batteries charged, so that when sickness comes we will have strength to endure.

Some years ago, a preacher had a prolonged illness in which he discovered that the truths he had believed through the years were not as helpful as he thought they would be. He visualized the gospel as a giant balloon with great lifting power—*if only he had the strength to hold onto the ropes!* But that was precisely his problem. He was sick and weak. He could not hold on.

We have had the same false perception of the gospel for too long. We say that the gospel has great power to lift, to rescue, to transform, if we can only believe and trust enough. Someone ought to get a giant needle and poke a hole in that balloon. Someone ought to let the hot air out (that is all it is filled with) and let it crumple to the ground at our feet. Then we can entrust our weight to Christ, whose everlasting arms will bear us up.

What is the essence of our belief in God? Is it our strength to "hang on to the ropes" of God's grace?

What is the essence of prayer? Is it our ability to prevail upon the dull ears of an inattentive God until we persuade him to come to our rescue?

How do we become strong? Is it by controlling our lives and offering them to God? Or is it by being willing to "let go and let God have his wonderful way"?

Such letting go does not mean that we cease all effort to grow in Christ. It does not spell the end of responsible Christian living. Actually, it frees us to engage in creative efforts of the best kind.

A student is struggling with a research project that isn't going well; a young businessman is struggling with a temptation he has often yielded to; a mother faces the task of finding work while raising small children. To these persons Christ says, "Let go. I will do this. I am your strength." Does the student push back his chair with a sigh of relief and wait for the Holy Spirit to type his paper? Would the businessman stop fighting against the Tempter? Would the mother gratefully spend the morning in bed? I think not.

A news magazine reporter followed Mother Teresa through her rounds among the poor and dying of Calcutta. He could scarcely keep up with her. "How are you able to keep this pace and do this incredible work?" he asked.

"I do nothing," she replied. "He does it all."

The poor man was totally bewildered. But she understood perfectly the open secret of strength. It is the secret of depending upon the One whose strength is inexhaustible.

When Christ tells us that he will be our strength, it may seem that nothing changes. Our work must go on. Our effort is still required. Yet everything changes. Our release to Jesus means the end of the destructive stress of self-dependence. New energy, creativity, and concentration are possible because the center of attention is the project at hand—not our pride. Our fear of failure is replaced with faith and trust in the strength of Christ.

Some Christians are saying, "I am strong. I can handle my life. I can get my act together and work things out, if I have a little time." But the word of the Lord is, "Give it up. Give your reputation to me. Let go of your self-dependency, and trust the strength that is inexhaustible."

Others are saying, "I am weak. I want to be strong, but I am not. I don't think I can make it." The word of the Lord is, "Give it up.

Surrender to me your inadequacy, weakness, and inability. I am your strength."

And others are saying, "I have to be strong for this time of crisis in my life" or "I must be strong for my children/father/mother/wife/husband" or "I'm going to be strong to handle this new situation with its new responsibilities." There is a word from the Lord: You do not have to be strong. He is strong. Give it to him.

In Christ there is forgiving grace for bad sinners and for good sinners, for Jews and for Gentiles. "There is no distinction; since all have sinned and fall short of the glory of God, they are justified by his grace as a gift, through the redemption which is in Christ Jesus" (Rom. 3:22–24). In Christ there is strengthening grace, both for strong Christians and weak Christians. There is no distinction in his sight. We are one in our humanity and one in our sin; we are one in receiving the forgiving grace of God in Jesus. We are one in our weakness and inability, and one in the strengthening grace of Christ, who is himself our strength.

In chapter 1 we talked about a shift in the spiritual center of gravity, away from ourselves to God. That is the open secret of strength that Paul points to throughout Philippians. Notice his outline:

Chapter 1: The Life of Christ
Chapter 2: The Mind of Christ
Chapter 3: The Goal of Christ
Chapter 4: The Strength of Christ

In each case, he calls us to release ourselves to Christ. As we experience the life of Christ, we know the death of our own false and ego-centered lives. As we have the mind of Christ, we surrender our self-serving attitudes and enter the Jesus way of thinking. As we pursue the goal of Christ, we must forget what is behind us and strive for what lies ahead. And as we experience the strength of Christ, we surrender our self-dependency to his lordship.

No, strong Christians are not innately strong persons. They have simply discovered they have no strength in themselves and have submitted themselves to Christ. In him they have found a strength that is inexhaustible. All Christians find strength as they learn to lean on him.

"I know how to be abased, and I know how to abound," Paul says. "In any and all circumstances I have learned the secret of facing plenty and hunger, abundance and want. I can do all things in him who strengthens me" (Phil. 4:12–13).

• Discussion Questions

1. Paul is in prison and obviously cannot "do all things." So what does he mean by this phrase?
2. For what particular situation in your life do you need to be strong?
3. Put in your own words Paul's secret of strength.
4. Do you agree that Christians with strong personalities are not necessarily strong Christians? What's the difference?
5. List some ways in which the development of spiritual strength is different from the development of physical strength. List some ways they are alike.
6. How would you define spiritual strength? According to your definition, do we ever become strong? Discuss.
7. Many Christians say they were glad they were "prayed up" when they faced a sudden emergency. How do you respond to this statement?
8. The balloon illustration shows the way many people understand the Christian life—that is, you have to try hard to be a Christian. Do you see it this way? Explain.
9. Imagine Christ saying to you in your present situation, "You don't have to be strong for this. I will be your strength." What would that change? What would it not change?